PROPHECY AND FULFILLMENT

and

GOD, MIND, CONSCIOUSNESS

PROPHECY AND FULFILLMENT
Address of 1939

and

GOD, MIND, CONSCIOUSNESS
Address of 1940

by

MARTHA WILCOX

The Bookmark
Santa Clarita, California

Library of Congress Number: 2004103889

Wilcox, Martha.
  Prophecy and fulfillment: address of 1939 ; and,
God, mind, consciousness : address of 1940 / Martha
Wilcox.
  p. cm.
  ISBN 0-930227-62-X

  1. Christian Science--Doctrines. 2. Prayer.
3. Consciousness--Religious aspects--Christianity.
I. Title. 11. Title: God, mind, consciousness.

BX6945W55 2004   289.5
                                  QB104-200045

Published by
The Bookmark
Post Office Box 801143
Santa Clarita, California 91380

CONTENTS

FOREWORD

Spiritual healing and regeneration come through prayer in Christian Science. This subjective experience brings about a greater understanding of God and man in His likeness. It is a spiritual conviction that whatever is true and right in any situation is already established through the operation of the divine Principle, Love. This divine intelligence must be expressed in human experience as we gain a better understanding of God. As this understanding unfolds we find true health and harmony.

These two addresses by Martha Wilcox, written for her association of students, explain how practical prayer can be in transforming consciousness and meeting our every need. She tells how prayer is the scientific means for bringing to light the spiritual nature of God and man. Underlying the many subjects in her discussion is this deep insight into the mental nature of all things, and how Christian Science enables us to exchange the false material belief for the spiritual idea that reflects the one Mind.

Whatever the subject, she always puts it into the mental realm and explains that healing or change must take place there if we are to overcome sin, sickness, disease and death. When through prayer we spiritualize our thinking, that *is* the healing. It is a spiritual law that this improved state of mind must objectify itself in improved health and well being. It all takes place subjectively, and Christian Science supplies the truth that brings about this inner change.

Mrs. Wilcox's writings are among the finest in explaining the form of prayer that spiritualizes consciousness. In reading her works we are assured that we are already living in the spiritual realm, one with God. Our only need is to see through the veil of matter into this heavenly kingdom, and this transformation takes place through scientific prayer.

PROPHECY AND FULFILLMENT
Association Address of 1939

PROPHECY AND FULFILLMENT
Association Address of 1939

by

Martha Wilcox

The Purpose of Our Association Meetings

Students, may I again remind you of Mrs. Eddy's purpose in establishing the Christian Science pupils' association as an activity in the Christian Science movement. An association meeting is quite different from a lecture. A lecture presents Christian Science to an audience in all states and stages of growth — it is given both to the illumined and unillumined mind — while in an association the work is presented to class-taught students only, or to the enlightened and educated minds of Christian Scientists.

The intent of an association meeting is the furtherance of class instruction, and the elucidation of the deep metaphysics found in the Bible, in our textbook, and in Mrs. Eddy's other writings. Each successive association meeting should keep pace with the advancement of the Christian Science movement; or in other words the students of the association should keep abreast of the continuous rise in thought, which is the unfoldment of the revelation of divine Science in human consciousness. The work should be in the nature of instruction and enlightenment, and should be basic in its application to the problems of the hour.

So today we are here for a renewal or a revival in the truth of our being, and for further spiritual education concerning our immortality. We cannot hear the words of Truth too often. If we have become dulled by reason of the pressing error of these times, the words of Truth will cut through this mesmerism, and reassure our thought as to the spiritual facts of being and the power of Mind.

The words of Truth are not mere repetitions, but are constant restatements. Our 'knowing the truth' is a continuous restatement of Truth, clung to and trusted. And what does the word of Truth do except demesmerize thought, and bring to light man's present immortality?

Unless life is becoming clearer and richer to us, we are not progressing as we should. And today I trust that we shall open our thought to a larger inpouring of the letter and the spirit of Truth, so that we may free our thought from its belief in perishable mortality, and plant it more firmly in the fact of our immortality.

1. PROPHECY AND FULFILLMENT

We are very much aware that the whole world at this present time is going through an experience of great significance, equal to none other since the advent of Jesus. It is important in view of the severe chemicalization which is going on in the world today, that we as Christian Scientists understand what is occurring, and through this understanding be the light of the world, a city that cannot be hid.

Mrs. Eddy says in *Science and Health with Key to the Scriptures*, "Science only can explain the incredible good and evil elements now coming to the surface." And she adds, "Mortals must find refuge in Truth in order to escape the error of these latter days." She also says, "The Science of Mind needs to be understood. Until it is understood, mortals are more or less deprived of Truth." Christian Scientists must have a higher altitude of thought than the use of personal opinions as their weapons. She also says, "Nothing is more antagonistic to Christian Science than a blind belief without understanding, for such a belief hides Truth and builds on error."

The events of this present time are of great significance to the Christian Science movement in view of the fact that certain prophecies in Mrs. Eddy's writings are becoming manifest in concrete phenomena. These questions are often asked: In what way are individual Christian Scientists related to the events that are taking place today? Do we as Christian Scientists have an individual responsibility in connection with these unusual phenomena?

The event of this day is the coming of the Son of God, visible humanly as the "Son of man coming . . . with power and great glory." The event of this day is the appearing of our divinity, made visible as a purer humanity. Our individual relation to this event is that we are the event itself.

The individual Christ, or the reality of individual man, is becoming appreciable to the world as our true humanhood. In other words, our divinity, which is ever at hand in power and great glory, is becoming visible in human manifestation.

The present event is none other than the great influx of the impersonal Christ or understanding, taking place in the consciousness of men and women; and the definite result of this influx of the impersonal Christ or understanding — which is a living, conscious, irresistible power — is the great upheaval and disturbance which is taking place in human consciousness as the mental atmosphere of the human being is cleared.

Let us remember that each individual human being is a mode of consciousness, or he is a mental world; and this upheaval that is taking place within himself, or within his own mental world, is the result of the conflict that is taking place between his real self — the Christ understanding — and his false educated beliefs.

It is well to remember that all the phenomena that are seen in our world today, are formed within our own consciousness and are wholly mental. All the sin and war and greed and earthquakes that we seem to experience at this time, are phenomena formed by the human mind and take place within the human consciousness of the individual. The upheaval and disturbance of this present day is the result of mankind shaking loose and clearing away his false beliefs; it is the dissolving of the false educated beliefs of the centuries — beliefs that have constituted much of the mental atmosphere of mortals.

It is said that at one time, when some great revelation of Truth was appearing in Mrs. Eddy's consciousness, she heard it thunder. Then she knew that established beliefs in the human mind were being uprooted and displaced.

Our responsibility at the present time is to have the spiritual discernment of the Son of God, which is the reality of all things as being at hand — even though "seen through a glass darkly," and not to be mesmerized with the noise and confusion of the passing away of that which is false belief only.

As Christian Scientists, we understand that the oneness of God and man is demonstrable in human experience. This oneness means that God and man is the one consciousness ever conscious of itself; it means that everything is in consciousness now — is here now. There can be no 'there' in consciousness.

There is nothing external to consciousness to change or to deal with or to be afraid of. There is no time, no waiting for things to be better, no process by which to make them better. There is nothing going on outside of consciousness; and all that is going on as consciousness is Mind consciously being man and the universe.

All things which appear to be transpiring as our world or consciousness, whether at home or abroad, whether the affairs of nations, national or international, are not outside of us where they would be difficult to handle, but are all here in consciousness, as realities, and they should be so understood — in their reality.

In infinite consciousness there is neither Jew nor Greek, there is neither bond nor free, there is neither male nor female, for we are all one in Christ Jesus. This means that there is no Jew, no Greek, no bond, no free, anywhere, because there is no 'there' in consciousness. All these in their true depiction are the sons and daughters of God — imperfectly known by us because of material

6

sense. Mrs. Eddy says, "Material sense defines all things materially." Scientific Christianity demands that we not only affirm that what we see humanly is the reality or the Son of God here and now, but that we demonstrate this Truth instead of merely believing in it, and demonstrate it to be a present fact here and now. This is our responsibility as individual Christian Scientists.

Biblical Prophecies

Many men of vision and great thinkers — seers of this age — are seeing the signs of the fulfillment in the latter part of this twentieth century, of certain Scriptural prophecies. One of these is recorded in the twentieth chapter of Exodus. It reads as follows: "Six days shalt thou labour, and do all thy work: But the seventh day is the sabbath of the LORD thy God: in it thou shalt not do any work."

In this prophecy which is at the beginning of Bible history, man is allotted six days in which to dispel the darkened sense which he himself created, when he erringly assumed his separation from God and seemed to wander far from true consciousness. To "labour, and do all thy work" signifies that during this period of six days man is to dispel the ignorance and the false beliefs which constitute so-called mortal mind or material sense, for by so doing he returns or is restored to his Father's house or true consciousness. St. Peter in his Second Epistle emphasizes the fact that "one day is with the Lord as a thousand years." Therefore, inasmuch as four thousand years elapsed from the time of this prophecy at the beginning of Bible history to the advent of Jesus on earth, and nearly two thousand years since Christ Jesus delivered the great influx of spiritual light and illumination which aided mankind to work out his salvation, obviously the six thousand years, or the six days spoken of in this prophecy, will end with our present twentieth century.

Then cometh the seventh, or the sabbath day — the day of rest from our labors, which is called the millennium. Particularly

7

during the past few years since the coming of Christian Science, great numbers are accepting and living the teachings of Jesus and are putting into practice the good which is theirs by divine right. We are fast awakening to the fact that nothing has changed us from being what we are — the sons and daughters of God. Is not this a time for great rejoicing?

In this present day, many who have spiritual discernment are seeing and experiencing the fulfillment of Jesus' prophecy regarding these latter days. Jesus prophesied these troubled times. He said, "Upon the earth distress of nations, with perplexity; . . . men's hearts failing them for fear, and for looking after those things which are coming on the earth: for the powers of heaven shall be shaken."

It should be observed that the words, "The powers of heaven shall be shaken," do not refer to the real heavens, but merely to the false sense of security which human beings have built up for themselves and now find to be utterly unstable. We are learning that a material concept of things is always an insecure concept.

What is to be our attitude toward these latter days? Surely not one of fear and anxiety and confusion. No! Jesus' admonition to us was that we ascend upon our housetop, meaning an altitude of understanding, and not come down. He also said in connection with this prophecy, "In your patience possess ye your souls," and, "there shall not an hair of your head perish."

Jesus' promise for these troubled times was, "Then shall they see the Son of man coming in a cloud with power and great glory." He also left for us the specific admonition, "And when these things begin to come to pass, then look up, and lift up your heads [understanding]; for your redemption draweth nigh." Yes, we have the unfailing assurance of rest and deliverance from what seems to be upheaval and disaster.

What is the Son of man, and what is his coming in a cloud with power and great glory? The Son of man is the Son of God perceived humanly. Mrs. Eddy says in *Miscellaneous Writings*,

"The human manifestation of the Son of God was called the Son of man, or Mary's son."

The Son of God and the Son of man are not two separate entities, but one. The Son of man is the Son of God imperfectly known because seen through the lens of material sense. The Son of man and the Son of God is the human and the divine coincidence that was seen in the man Jesus. What appears to us to be a human being, is in his real character deific, and is the Son of God. And if we fully understood ourselves and others, as being the Son of God, we would all be seen as having the power and great glory that Jesus had, and we would demonstrate it.

Jesus asked his disciples, "Whom say ye that I [the Son of man] am?" And the discerning Simon Peter answered and said, "Thou art the Christ, the Son of the living God."

This spiritual fact has been revealed to us, and we should ask ourselves, are we, at least in a measure, demonstrating that "now are we the sons of God?" Are we demonstrating that each one of us is now the individual Christ-self, seen humanly or seen in his true humanhood?

The coming of the Son of man "in a cloud with power and great glory" refers to the demonstration of Christian Science — which demonstration is the Son of man. The coming in a cloud signifies that the demonstration is often mysterious to mortal mind and yet the power and glory of it is recognized.

Why Sickness and Sin Seem Aggravated

If sickness seems to be aggravated in these days, it is because we are passing out of the hour when we shall be sick and need healing into the hour when the Son of God — the reality of all things — will so occupy consciousness, that what appears to need healing will be revealed as divine idea, which always has been whole and complete. Are we not ready today to leave the belief of sickness, without attempting in some way to heal it or to destroy it?

How can we heal that which is already whole if we see it as it already is? Let us remember Jesus' words, "I am not come to destroy, but to fulfill." This means that we fulfill by seeing perfectly a reality which as yet appears imperfectly.

If sin seems to be aggravated in these days, it is because the dream of corporeality and materiality — the dream of mistakes and frailties and imperfections and failures, and the suffering for all of them — is dissolving. These are beliefs only. Because of the revelation that "now are we the sons of God," are we not ready to dismiss these beliefs without trying to regenerate and destroy that which is nothing?

What if in the dream of material sense our sins were as scarlet? In reality, and that is all there ever has been to us, we were and are as white as snow. What if in the dream our sins and failures and mistakes were red like crimson? There never was an instant of eternity when the sons and daughters of God were not white as wool.

No matter what the nature of the dream or the seeming time it has continued, it is only a dream without a dreamer. The hour is passing when we desire to have the condition of our dream fixed up, and then continue our dreaming. The hour is come when we are awakening to our sense of wholeness — we are stepping out of the dream, not just fixing it up.

In this hour of the coming of the Son of man in power and great glory, men and women — Christian Scientists — are arising in thought as never before, recognizing their true state of being. As the prodigal son "came to himself," so we are coming to ourselves, finding ourselves, knowing ourselves. The time has come when we can present ourselves to the world in the highest human manifestation of the sons and daughters of God, which will be the Son of man or our true humanhood. And our reality, the Son of God or the individual Christ, will evidence Himself in His divine character — power and great glory.

The dream — that which is nothing — has not changed us,

nor can it change us from being who we are and what we are, even the sons and daughters of God and joint heirs with Jesus Christ. "Ye are all the children of light, and the children of the day: Ye are not of the night, nor of darkness."

Mrs. Eddy's Prophecies

In Mrs. Eddy's writings, we find many prophecies concerning the closing years of the twentieth century. In *Pulpit and Press*, she quotes, "History shows the curious fact that the closing years of every century are years of more intense life, manifested in unrest or in aspiration, and scholars of special research . . . assert that the end of a cycle is marked by peculiar intimations of man's immortal life."

We hear much in these days about immortal life. Christian Scientists should intelligently reason out that life is a scientific fact — is diseaseless and ageless and endless and deathless. Such statements of truth do not just happen to be spoken. They are not of the personal mind, but they are the appearing of the Son of God as the Son of man in human consciousness.

Mrs. Eddy makes a remarkable prophecy concerning the church of this twentieth century. In *Pulpit and Press* she says, "If the lives of Christian Scientists attest their fidelity to Truth, I predict that in the twentieth century every Christian church in our land, and a few in far-off lands, will approximate the understanding of Christian Science sufficiently to heal the sick in his name. Christ will give to Christianity his new name, and Christendom will be classified as Christian Scientists."

This is a remarkable prediction. Someone may say, It does not look much like it now; but we must remember that prophecy is the foretelling of the appearing of that which is already finished and complete.

Jesus said, "For as the lightning cometh out of the east, and shineth even unto the west; so shall the coming of the Son of man be." The one Holy Church, the universal Christ, the Son of God, is everywhere, universal, now appearing as the Son of man, the highest that the human mind can appreciate. What can hinder what He doeth?

In *Pulpit and Press*, Mrs. Eddy also says, "When the doctrinal barriers between the churches are broken and the bonds of peace are cemented by spiritual understanding and Love, there will be unity of spirit, and the healing power of Christ will prevail. Then shall Zion have put on her most beautiful garments, and her waste places budded and blossomed as the rose."

Mrs. Eddy makes another momentous prophecy, the fulfillment of which is appearing at this present time. This prophecy concerns "The New Woman." Before Jesus' time women were considered of lower rank and lesser intelligence than men. All the patriarchs and prophets were seers and were supposed to attain much wisdom, and this wisdom was recognized as the masculine element in consciousness. Then, according to prophecy, there appeared a woman, Mary, who brought to mankind that which was even greater than wisdom, or the masculine element. She brought to mankind "the light of the world," illustrating the feminine element in consciousness, which is love. The world calls this present time 'Woman's Day.' Since the Christian era began, woman has steadily risen to the heights where she now stands. Today women compel the attention of the world, for they have reached the side of men in nearly every endeavor, and are destined to succeed fully in this century.

Before the close of these six days in which we are to labor and do all our work, we shall see woman standing beside man — his rightful equal — for so she was created.

But in Mrs. Eddy's prophecy of woman, 'Woman's Day' typifies the day of the fullness of Love. Mrs. Eddy is not referring to corporeal woman or the female gender. Woman typifies the female element in consciousness, the female of God's creating, the fullness of Love. The female element in consciousness is that irresistible Love which ends wars, cancels all misunderstanding, transcends all fears and limitations, scales the heights and reaches the mount of God, who is Love itself.

'Woman's Day' typifies a state of consciousness wherein Life and Love, man and woman, are seen as one being, not two, and a new state of living begins. Mrs. Eddy has predicted that in this present time there will be a marked appearing of the feminine characteristic to thought — the love characteristic of thought which gave birth to Jesus, and later to the revelation of Christian Science.

Love, or the feminine element in consciousness, is higher than the masculine element and so encompasses the masculine, as illustrated by Mary and Jesus. The Virgin Mary, (woman) gave birth to Jesus (man). This is the day when Love — the feminine element — will encompass the masculine and they will be one, humanly speaking. The woman thought will rise to see herself as man — the full representation of God — and they will be one and that one perfect. When the misconception of male and female first appeared in man's thought, it was the belief that masculine and feminine elements of consciousness were two separate states, instead of a unit wherein and whereof Life and Love combine to operate as one. The male and female of God's creating are never to be thought of as though they were two entities, distinct from each other, but must always be seen as one inseparable being.

This is the day when the female characteristic of thought will understand and be her individual Christ-self, and she will love all men and women and things as her individual Christ-self. This state of thought is surely unselfish and is the love that thinketh no evil.

That old saying, 'Only that day dawns to which we are awake' is true. And at this present time, we need to be very much awake and alert to what is actually transpiring in our mental world. He that hath eyes — that is, spiritual discernment — sees the mist of material beliefs dissolving and the kingdom of heaven come on earth.

2. THE MILLENNIUM — THE "GREATER WORKS"

The fulfillment of prophecy always seems remote, just as it did in the days of the coming of Jesus. But if we had eyes to see, we would perceive that the fulfillment of prophecy is but the appearing in consciousness of that which is already in existence. The millennium is appearing now, and will appear in its full significance at the time that prophecy has fixed for its appearing. The millennium will appear just as Christ Jesus appeared, at the time prophesied, and as the revelation of Christian Science appeared in fulfillment of prophecy.

We do not think that as the hour strikes at midnight in the year 1999, that we shall awaken in the millennium or in an entirely different state of consciousness; but Christian Scientists and great thinkers believe that the millennium is appearing now; and that in the closing years of this century, it will have appeared in great significance.

According to the dictionary, the millennium is a period of a thousand years as mentioned in the twentieth chapter of Revelation, during which time holiness is to be triumphant. Hence, it is a period of great happiness, good government and freedom from wickedness. Some believe that during this period Christ will reign on earth in person.

All Christian Scientists understand that Christ is not a person, but is the impersonal truth about everything and everyone that we now know humanly and materially. The millennium is that period in which the impersonal Christ, or the Son of God, is appearing on earth, or in human consciousness, as the Son of man. It is that period of consciousness in which men and women are coming into their true humanhood.

In Christian Science we learn that Christ, the Son of God, is the divine actuality of all existing persons and things. And, according to prophecy, this divine actuality of all persons and things is now appearing in concrete phenomena as the Son of man in power and great glory — which means that divine actualities with their power and glory, are appearing in the highest forms appreciable to human consciousness.

To a Christian Scientist, the millennium will be the state of his own individual consciousness. It will be his freedom to think without the constraint of the so-called mortal mind, for as long as our thought is constrained, just that long is divine power lacking. When we are free to think divinely, without the constraint of mortal mind, then we are free to act divinely, without constraint. Then we can walk over the waves, calm the storm, and feed the multitude, if need be.

The infinite God-mind seems to be hidden because we seem to have a mind of our own, but as thought attains something of its right origin — the divine Mind — then the power, the omnipotence of good, is available to us, and we shall naturally do the "greater works" that the Master said we would do. (See John 14:12.)

Only those who have spiritual discernment realize what is taking place and the import of the present time. Those of discernment realize that the world is passing out of one mental cycle, or mode of thinking and living, into another cycle of enlarged thinking and better living, and of spiritual power. When this great moral chemicalization has done its work, we shall find error destroyed, and we shall discern good only at hand. And in the meantime, we should understand that what appears so distressing in this present day, is not crucifixion, but resurrection.

The following question was asked in the 1937 Metaphysical College Normal Class: "Is the world situation a chemicalization brought about by the revelation and demonstration of Christian Science, and is it so severe that it is destroying rather than redeeming?"

The teacher, Mr. Bicknell Young's answer was: "We cannot say that Christian Science demonstration, as partially appearing, produces chemicalization that will destroy rather than redeem;

but we can take the attitude that Christian Science demonstrated by you and me does not chemicalize beyond our ability to take care of the chemicalization. So if your thought takes on something of the grandeur of God, that will take care of the situation. (See *Science and Health* 401:7-20.) If Mind takes care of the situation, we can do something more practical than answer the question. As the terror that seems so intense in other nations disappears, the evil itself will disappear. When we see it as God sees it, its terrors begin to disappear. If God were demonstrated this instant, the error would have no terror, because we would recognize what is actually going on. As Christian Scientists, we should not make evil either real or personal, but we should not ignore it. Christian Scientists have a responsibility in this matter, because Truth has been revealed to them."

The Christian Scientist realizes that his consciousness, which is his world — with its people, its religions, its governments and politics — is within himself, and that it depends largely upon himself whether his world is the kingdom of heaven or a misconception of the kingdom of heaven.

Every Christian Scientist should know the nothingness of Fascism and Communism, for both would bind us so that we could not think, and human beings must be free to think. Anything that threatens free thought is dangerous, and we should demonstrate its nothingness.

The Passing Away of Matter and Mortal Mind

According to prophecy and actual experience, this is the day when much mortal mind and materiality is passing away, and it is passing away with much noise and disturbance. And all this is taking place within the individual's own consciousness or he could not be aware of it, although it all seems to be taking place external to him. The discerning Peter foretold this day. He said, "But the day of the Lord will come as a thief in the night; in the which the

16

heavens shall pass away with a great noise, and the elements shall melt with fervent heat, the earth also and the works that are therein shall be burned up."

Our world to a great extent is mentalized; that is, people in general believe that everything of which they are conscious is mental. But in the millennium a greater work than mentalization will be consummated. Then the world and everything of which the world consists will be spiritualized. And, students, it is the duty of every Christian Scientist to see that this greater work is active in his individual consciousness in this present day.

As students of Christian Science we are learning that we do not change our world simply by transposing it from a material world to a mental or thought world; we are learning that in order to see our world as spiritual instead of material, we must set aside that which is causing the material sense of our world. The people, things, and conditions of our world seem to be material, because so-called mortal mind's concept of itself and all that it is, is always matter. Mortal mind sees and feels itself as matter; its objectifications are matter. The seeming material world is mortal mind as it is to itself.

What is matter? Matter is the primal concept of mortal mind; matter is the mortal, perishable sense of that which is imperishable. Matter is a misstatement; it is a delusion, an illusion, a deception. But in the millennium, we shall see the people and all things of our world in a truer depict, and realize that they are God-being and are spiritual.

We, who are students of Christian Science, understand and demonstrate the greater works. We are proving that all things of which our world consists, are God's creation, and have always been actualities of Spirit. They only appear material or mortally mental because we still see them through the lens of false material sense.

Let it be clearly understood that we do not spiritualize matter, because matter is not some thing or condition to be dealt with, to be fulfilled or to be destroyed. Matter is a deception; it is a false

17

appearance of an actuality at hand. The actuality does not need to be spiritualized, and matter is not something which can be spiritualized. Rather do we dematerialize these actualities by removing from them the false appearance or material accompaniments — the false sense of density, weight, finiteness and impermanence. We, as Christian Scientists, have done much dematerialization up to the present time. Yes, we have come a long way on our journey from sense to Soul. It is difficult to conceive just how far we have come since we began our six days of labor, and to what extent we are equipped to do the greater works.

Let us consider just how much of the statement, "he that believeth on me, the works that I do shall he do also," has been fulfilled, and see if we are not more fully qualified to do the greater works than the false sense of humility is permitting us to admit. When we first took up the study of Christian Science, it was largely for personal improvement — either to gain health, harmony or supply — and that was perfectly legitimate at that stage of our growth; but it is a far greater work to do what we are now doing — demonstrating our oneness with God, our oneness with all good; demonstrating that man as idea or reflection already has health, harmony and supply and could not be without them. The thought of Christian Scientists has been vastly improved in the understanding of the Science of Mind and its application to our human needs. Our thought has been gradually educated to the apprehension of things as they really are.

The Coincidence of the Human and Divine

At the time of coming into Christian Science, about the only thing we were sure of was that we were alive, and that we existed as human beings. At that time we believed that human beings were mortals, and that somehow through Christian Science mortals would become immortals; we believed that mortal mind was an entity, and that somehow it was to be transformed into a divine Mind; we also believed that what God had called "good" and "very good" had lapsed into evil, and that there must be regeneration and restoration.

But now we understand and prove that what appears to be ourselves as a human being, is not a mortal, but is our divine self appearing; and because our divine self — the only self here — is imperfectly known because seen through the lens of material sense, it appears to our sight and sense as a human being. It is clearly seen that we have some discernment of the divine fact of ourselves at hand, or we would not be conscious of ourselves as even a human being.

As the mist of ignorance about God and man thins, our divine self appears in truer depict or as a better sense of man. This is our true humanhood appearing as the millennium or true consciousness, in which man is as sinless as his Maker. Our true humanhood is from above, never of mortal mind. Our true humanhood is not a mortal man at any stage of its appearing. We should never consider ourselves a mortal. We are never other than the divine man appearing in fuller degree. Our true humanhood, or divine self, will never disappear, but will appear from glory to glory unto its completeness and perfection. Herein is the coincidence of the human and divine as exemplified in Christ Jesus.

Is it not a far greater work to understand our divinity to be at hand than to believe that man is a mortal who can sin, suffer and die, and must be healed and saved? So-called mortal mind expressed as mortal man is a myth — a state of deception — and is not an entity to be healed and saved. The so-called human being is already the divine self, and it surely does not need healing and saving. All good, all actualities, have never lapsed into evil, and they need no restoration.

All there is to what constitutes me humanly is now the divine, imperfectly known. All is now reality. All are now actualities. All is now Deity. All is I AM Himself, being all formations as divine ideas. Therefore ideas have never been matter nor separated from their divine Principle. They never need to be healed; they need only to be revealed in their perfection.

We do not believe that a mortal ever becomes an immortal, or that evil ever becomes good. Good already is, and is all. Good is what we are demonstrating; and it is not material, but is spiritual good — now. Mortal mind does not increase in wisdom, knowledge and understanding; but wisdom, knowledge and understanding decrease the beliefs of mortal mind until it disappears.

Everything that we call 'better' is not better because mortal mind is better, but because mortal mind is disappearing and more of reality is appearing. Whenever illumination appears, that illumination is divine being or reality better seen. We do not coalesce with mortal mind, but we set it aside. Mortal mind does not and cannot improve; it disappears; and the thing appearing is the divine idea unfolding.

Our Progress

During the years that I have been in Christian Science, the thought of Christian Scientists, and coincidentally the thought of the whole world, has vastly improved in understanding and method. It was not so long ago that some practitioners and teachers said, "You haven't any hand." They said this because they believed that the hand which you now have is material; and since *Science and Health* emphatically states, "There is no matter," they believed the hand that you have is matter, and took the position that you had no hand.

It took Mrs. Eddy some time to reveal the truth on this particular point, even to those who thought they had quite an altitude of understanding. She made it clear that matter is a misstatement, a misconception, a false appearance only, of the actuality at hand. She made it clear that as the misconception is dissolved, the actuality, though imperfectly seen and known, is the only thing present. Mrs. Eddy told Mr. Kimball and others who taught in the Metaphysical College to instruct those who were to be sent out as teachers into the field, that anything that exists is never matter at any time, but is a divine idea of Mind and is not to be destroyed, but fulfilled.

The impersonal Truth unfolded into another period of clearer understanding, and certain teachers announced that the organs and functions of our present body are spiritual — are divine ideas consciously unfolding. How mortal mind resisted this unfoldment of Truth, and everyone who made these statements was accused of spiritualizing matter! Mortal mind said they were trying to make material organs into realities, or divine ideas. It was and is amazing to see how mortal mind clung and still clings tenaciously to itself as matter. To mortal thought matter was something, and to admit that it was only an illusion, a misstatement, or a deception would have been its own undoing.

But at this present stage of illumination or understanding in human consciousness, the students of Christian Science do not hesitate to say that what appears to be matter is Spirit; that the so-called organs of our present body are ideas, actualities — are Spirit itself being spiritual formations. We understand and prove that our present body and all that constitutes our present body, even though it is regarded as matter, is demonstrated to be spiritual or Spirit expressed.

Today we understand that what appears to be matter is Spirit in expression. Spirit and matter are not two, but one. Mrs. Eddy says good and evil "are not two but one, for evil is naught, and good only is reality." When we see evil, we are seeing good in reversion; and when death appears to our sense, we are seeing Life in reversion.

The "Greater Works"

Do we not see how true thinking has been expanding and ascending naturally, until it has resulted in the greater works? This ascendancy of thought has not been personal thinking, but has been the unfoldment of the Christ as individual man.

Someone may think, How can there be greater works than the work of Jesus? Can there be anything greater than healing the sick instantaneously, making the blind to see, the deaf to hear, the lame to walk, the dead to live, and all instantly? Can there be greater works than these? Jesus himself said so, and that we should do them.

Jesus said, "He that believeth on me, the works I do shall he do also; and greater works than these shall he do; because I go unto my Father." This "I" that went unto the Father did not mean a personal I. The I, or Ego, of anyone is always Truth. This I, or Truth, of Jesus turned to God absolutely. This I, or Truth, of Jesus did not turn to any person or to a personal self, but went unto his Father — Truth. So, in order that we do the greater works, the I of us must go to our Father, Truth, absolutely.

In speaking of the healing work, Mrs. Eddy says, "This absolute demonstration of Science must be revived. . . A healing that is not guesswork . . . but instantaneous cure." (*Miscellaneous Writings*) At this time, according to prophecy, the Christ, the Son of God — the reality of all men and women and of all things — is appearing in human consciousness in such irresistible activity and power, and with such illumination of understanding, that ignorance of God and man and the universe is being swept away and the "new heaven and new earth" are being revealed.

These greater works are equivalent to no work to be done. If we start our thinking from the standpoint of having something to do, we shall never get it done. Mind declares itself and its manifestation. Man is as finished and complete as Mind itself. Man, as idea or reflection, has nothing to do but unfold in accord with his Maker.

Let us read again the prophecy from Exodus: "Six days shalt thou labor, and do all thy work: But the seventh day [the millennium] is the sabbath of the Lord thy God: in it thou shalt not do any work." The statement, thou shalt not do any work on the sabbath day, is not a command to us to cease work; but it is a revelation that in the millennium, or the sabbath day of the Lord, it will not be necessary to labor. The seventh day, or the millennium, is the climax of ascending thought wherein we realize the finished kingdom within us.

The coming of the millennium wherein there is harmony and peace is no idle dream. In *Miscellany*, Mrs. Eddy says of the millennium, "Its impetus, accelerated by the advent of Christian Science, is marked, and will increase till all men shall know Him (divine Love) from the least to the greatest, and one God and the brotherhood of man shall be known and acknowledged throughout the earth."

3. THE SOURCE, ORIGIN, AND POWER OF THOUGHT

All down the ages mortals have been imbued with the notion that they do their own thinking, and that the quality of their thinking is a personal matter; that thought depends upon a personal mind that is dualistic in nature, and can think both good and evil.

There is nothing that so deters our growth in Christian Science as the failure to understand the source and origin and power of thought. All Christian Scientists should fully understand that the human being's right thinking is not from a personal mind or a brain; neither is it a matter of habit; but it is a matter of being the reflection of the God-mind.

There is only one thinking agent, and that is the divine Mind, and the infinitude of Mind's thoughts or ideas is His expression or manifestation, and is man. Man never originates his thoughts, but man is the thoughts or ideas of the divine Mind. It should be emphatically understood that man does not originate his thinking, but man is the thinking that the divine Mind is being. Whatever thinking is going on, there is divine Mind in conscious operation as the unfoldment of thought or ideas.

Even if the thinking seems to be evil, the trouble is not with the thinking, but is with the lens through which it is seen. Those of us who are enlightened by Christian Science, understand that we are right scientific thought, and we understand the value of scientific thought. Little by little, we are learning that every so-called human problem can be worked through by keeping the source, origin, and power of all thought in the divine Mind.

We live in a world of thought pictures. All there is to one's world — which is one's self — is thought. All things, both animate and inanimate, which make up our consciousness, are thoughts or ideas. And since the source of all thought is the divine Mind, then all things are spiritual and real. Mrs. Eddy tells us that God's "thoughts are spiritual realities."

If we look at a white horse through green glasses, we sense a green horse. And, although the horse appears green, it still is a white horse. The green glasses do not create a green horse, but the green horse is really the green glasses, and will disappear with the glasses. (See *Science and Health* 397:23-32.)

Is There a Good Mind and an Evil Mind?

In Proverbs we read, "As [man] thinketh in his heart, so is he." And Jesus said, "Whatsoever thing from without entereth into the man, it cannot defile him; . . . That which cometh out of the man, that defileth the man." Paul speaks of the carnal mind as enmity against God, and he also exhorts the Philippians to, "Let this mind be in you, which was also in Christ Jesus."

Until the revelation of Christian Science, these Scriptural passages and many others, have been interpreted to mean that if a man thought evil thoughts, he had an evil mind of his own and was an evil man; but if his thoughts were good, he had a good mind of his own and was a good man. We can readily see that such interpretation separated the human being from God and gave as much entity or identity to a carnal mind as it gave to the divine Mind. This belief in two minds persisted until the revelation of Mary Baker Eddy that our present Mind is God. And now we are beginning to perceive that wherever there is mind — that is God; and if we see mind expressed as evil, we need to take off the green glasses.

Since Mind is God, it is infinite — is All, and this precludes the possibility of a carnal mind. With this inspired revelation which Mrs. Eddy gave to the world, our Bible has become a new book, and the teachings of Paul have taken on a new significance.

Because of Mrs. Eddy's revelation that Mind is God and infinite, the carnal or mortal mind has lost its identity as mind. Now the so-called carnal mind is considered, not as a mind that originates and enacts wrong thought, but as ignorance or false belief. Mrs. Eddy says in *Miscellaneous Writings*, "Matter [meaning the carnal or mortal mind] is a misstatement of Mind," just as much as two and two equals five is a misstatement of mathematics. Ignorance, false sense, false belief are the green glasses which can be removed only by gaining an understanding of the fact that Mind is God, manifested infinitely as all thoughts or ideas, which is man. This fact is to be demonstrated by each one of us.

With the revelation that Mind is God, and that man is the activity of Mind, or that man is the thinking that the God-mind is doing, humanity took a great step forward out of the maze wherein man was supposed to do his own thinking and could think both good and evil.

In the textbook Mrs. Eddy asks the question, "Is Mind capable of error as well as of truth, of evil as well as of good, when God is All and He is Mind and there is but one God, hence one Mind?" Again Mrs. Eddy says, "Mind is one, including noumenon and phenomena, God and His thoughts."

I am sure that you will fully agree with me, that since Mind is God and infinite, that Mind and His manifestation of thoughts is the "same yesterday, and today, and forever," and that infinity and its being and its manifestation — man — is wholly accomplished and finished now.

You will agree with me that the only Mind, here and everywhere — since it is infinite in its being and infinite in its expression, man — must be a state of conscious completeness and perfection. It is quite obvious that Mind could not disclose itself to itself, or disclose itself to its idea of itself — man — in progressive degrees of good or a part of good. If such a thing could be, Mind would, at some time, be less than whole or infinite; or less than complete; or less than being finished or accomplished; and His manifestation — man — would be a state of conscious incompleteness and imperfection.

God, our Mind, appears to be unfolding as our consciousness in progressive degrees of good, but this sense of less than completeness is because of our ignorance of God's and man's completeness.

The supposititious sense limitation or our limited sense of infinite good, is not mortal mind as an entity being this false sense; but this false sense is a result of ignorance; it is a negation; it is the absence of understanding on our part. Yes, it is the green glasses that need to be discarded. It is our ignorance or false sense which accounts for the one Mind, God, seeming to unfold as different states of consciousness, or as many minds. It is surely clear that there is no other mind to combat. It is our ignorance of the one infinite Mind which needs to be combated, and the only way to combat ignorance is to gain an understanding of the fact of God and man as one being.

Mrs. Eddy has given a name to this belief of limited consciousness, to this less than completeness. She calls it "mortal mind" and says, "The phrase mortal mind implies something untrue and therefore unreal; and as the phrase is used in teaching Christian Science, it is meant to designate that which has no real existence." (*Science and Health*)

So-called mortal mind, being no entity or no mind, is not conscious, therefore it is not a creator of thought or sense. The limited sense of good which it seems to produce is our ignorance of completeness; it is inversion; it is illusion; and there is no objectification to an illusion.

So-called mortal mind, being the ignorant or false sense of infinity, makes the divine Mind appear as both good and evil. If the understanding of the completeness of good were demonstrated by us individually, there could be only good. It is the ignorance of the completeness of good that is the sense of limitation or evil. Evil and ignorance are synonymous.

It is our limited awareness of good which denies or negatives the allness of God — the one Mind. Apparent evil is not evil as an entity; it is not something of itself, but is our imperfect apprehension of good. The so-called material universe is not a material universe, but is our limited sense of the spiritual universe.

It is basic to the demonstration of Christian Science that

27

we understand the character of so-called mortal mind as ignorance of God, the one Mind. When we once understand that so-called mortal mind cannot form a thought or a sensation, or even exist to itself, then we cease to fear it. It is not something that can act or do anything to us, any more than the ignorance of music can do something to us. Being ignorant of music merely deprives us of the experience of music.

Christian Scientists talk too much about mortal mind. They are apt to give the impression that it is something to combat, or that it is an evil entity to be overcome. The only way we can overcome the ignorance of music is to learn music, and to do this we need to give all our attention to getting an understanding of the principle of music.

We read in the textbook, "Evil is a negation, because it is the absence of truth. It is nothing, because it is the absence of something. It is unreal, because it presupposes the absence of God, the omnipotent and omnipresent. Every mortal must learn that there is neither power nor reality in evil."

Humanity has only to accept this revelation — that Mind is God, is one and is infinite, and through reason and logic demonstrate this as individual consciousness — in order to wipe out the seeming presence of less than one Mind or absence of Mind.

The Christ — the Activity of Divine Mind

Christian Scientists understand that God, the one conscious Mind, is unceasingly active as thought or ideas, and is intelligence. This unceasing activity of Mind as consciousness is the Christ, or is the thinking that constitutes all individual men and women.

This unceasing activity of Mind as true scientific thinking, or as the one intelligence, or as the Christ, was all there was to the mind of Jesus, and is all there is to the mind of any one of us. Every thought that constituted the mind of Jesus was the activity of the one Mind — as Christ, and his every thought had its source in divine Mind, and is the Christ, and is accompanied with almighty power. The reason for our apparent lack of divine power in this present day in our healing work, in our churches, in our business activities, is because we are ignorant of the source and character of the thinking that constitutes our present mind; otherwise we would have more of the power of the Holy Ghost.

Thought or thinking is the only thing going on in the universe, and it goes on unceasingly throughout eternity. Anything that exists is conscious Mind being that thought or idea. The unceasing activity of conscious Mind is the thinking, or ideas, that is His manifestation, or is man.

Thinking, if it is real thought, reflects Mind because it is conscious Mind being the thinking. When our thinking approximates the divine Mind, it is the divine Mind. There is no other mind to form thought or to think. When our thought approximates the divine Mind, it is Mind — the omnipotence of God made manifest as idea; then power — the omnipotence of good — is available to us in our human activities.

The demonstration of power is Mind's demonstration, and is in evidence when we have accepted that Mind and permitted our thinking to have its inception in that Mind. We should ever permit our thinking to be of the character of Deity or divine Mind.

In Christian Science, it is not we as a person thinking, but it is ever-conscious Mind being, and because of this, our thoughts are fast breaking away from the finite and expressing the infinite. One of the main objects of class instruction and our yearly association, is to gain that ascendancy of thought which was presented throughout the career of Christ Jesus and which culminated in his ascension into the consciousness of universal reality.

Mrs. Eddy writes in *Science and Health*, "A knowledge of the Science of being develops the latent abilities and possibilities of man. It extends the atmosphere of thought, giving mortals access to broader and higher realms. It raises the thinker into his native air of insight and perspicacity." Many students in the professional and business world have proved this statement of Mrs. Eddy's to be true, and every Christian Scientist is grateful for the Science of true thinking.

The Science of true thinking is lifting humanity out of petty mortal thinking towards the heights of infinite knowing, where the reflection of the boundless power of God constitutes our ability to think.

4. NO MALPRACTICE

Students, I would like you to carry in thought four scientific facts that will help you in the consideration of our next subject today: "No Malpractice."

First: Since Mind is one infinite self-conscious being, then everything in the universe exists because this Mind has unfolded itself out into all existing things — out into infinity.

Second: One infinite eternal Mind precludes the possibility of a lesser mind. Therefore so-called mortal mind is never an entity or a mind, but is that which has no existence — does not fill space. It is ignorance, or a false sense of the allness of God.

Third: We appear to sense things which we are not experiencing — which are not going on. For instance, we can sense that we are moving on a train that is standing still, or we can sense falling in our sleep. When we sense things which are not taking place at all, this illustrates what Mrs. Eddy terms false belief or false sense. Such is all mental malpractice. Mental malpractice is something that we sense, but which is not going on at all.

Fourth: We must bear in mind that one infinite consciousness is every individual's consciousness. We do not have a consciousness of our own, any more than an individual ray of light has light of its own. The one light of the sun is the light of every individual ray. Just so, Truth, being universal consciousness, is the consciousness of every individual. But malpractice claims to be a universal consciousness with everything in a sense of reversion. It claims that this universal false sense is the consciousness of every individual man and woman. This false claim is what we as Christian Scientists are to uncover as nothing and nobody. We often hear Christian Scientists say quite glibly, "There is no such thing as mental malpractice." But to know theoretically that there is no malpractice, and then talk and act as if there were such evil going on around us, is of no practical value to the student.

What is Mental Malpractice?

We should understand that mental malpractice is false sense only, and not something we are experiencing. Usually we believe that some person is thinking evilly about another person, thereby harming that person through this mental process. But mental malpractice is entirely impersonal — a person has nothing to do with this false sense, and to be effectually dealt with it must be so understood. Mrs. Eddy says in *Miscellaneous Writings*, "Not to know that a false claim is false, is to be in danger of believing it; hence the utility of knowing evil aright, then reducing its claim to its proper denominator, — nobody and nothing." So it is with the claim of malpractice; we need to know that it is utterly false — nobody and nothing — and then we are its master and not its servant.

So-called mortal mind, which is all there is to malpractice, is a lie, "a bland denial of Truth." It is the assumption that life is in matter and that man is personal and material. So-called mortal mind, ignorant of God and man as one being, causes the sense of the opposite of Truth, or causes mental malpractice. And mortal mind, or mental malpractice, cannot disappear until understanding, or the reality of all things, appears in consciousness.

There is no personal mind either as a claim or as a fact. What appears to us as many minds is the one infinite Mind disclosing itself infinitely. We have no mind which we alone possess, but the one universal God-mind is the Mind of each one of us. And because of our ignorance of this one universal impersonal God-mind, there seems to be the one universal impersonal claim of false consciousness appearing to us as many mortal minds.

Everything of which we are conscious constitutes our consciousness. Everything is mental and is really a form of spiritual sense. Everything of which we are conscious, even in belief, is truly a spiritual fact in consciousness. All sense testimony, — such as sensation of pain or pleasure, and all sense of form, color, substance and tangibility, are modes of consciousness, and when translated are the infinite spiritual senses of the one Mind. They are Mind consciously being. They originate in the God-mind and are never of the world — never of a person or of a body — no matter what false sense testimony says to the contrary.

Our world is purely a sense-world. All the circumstances, events and experiences of our world are transpiring as consciousness. Our present sense-world is in its actuality a spiritual sense-world; and as we overcome the belief of false sense, our present sense-world will appear progressively more real and substantial in the ratio that spiritual sense appears as our consciousness.

Individual and Universal Consciousness One

Our individual consciousness is in actuality a mode of absolute Truth, but at the present time, because of false sense, it appears relative rather than absolute. This is due to our ignorance of God and man as one being. At this present time in belief we are all relatively of one and the same sense of limited consciousness. Otherwise we would have no awareness of each other as we appear today; we would have no point of contact; and we would not have the same sense of our world.

Mortal mind, or the one universal false sense of things, is seemingly our individual false sense of things. Each of us seems to have a varying degree of one and the same universal false sense, and this results in mass false sense or mass mesmerism or mental malpractice. For example, my consciousness in its actuality is a living conscious sense of infinite good; but because of my ignorance of this fact there is the mental malpractice or the false sense of limitation. I may sense only five dollars, but because my individual consciousness in its reality is the spiritual sense of infinity, I have the assurance that this malpractice or sense of limitation can be set aside, and that it is possible for me to have many times five dollars.

Since each of us has a varying degree of one and the same false sense, J. D. Rockefeller sensed the same false limitation that I sensed. He, no doubt, sensed five million dollars, but because of conscious infinity at hand, he sensed that it was possible for him to have many times five million dollars. Both John D. Rockefeller and I had the same limitation, only in different degrees. This limited sense is not my personal sense, and it is not Mr. Rockefeller's personal sense, but it is false limited sense common to us all. It is mass sense or mass mesmerism or mental malpractice.

What appears as your world appears as my world. What appears as my personal disease is not personal but impersonal disease; what appears as anyone's personal hate, resentment or injustice is impersonal hate, resentment or injustice. The one universal false sense of disease, hate, resentment or injustice operates consciously or unconsciously as personal sense or mental malpractice.

My individual mind is my universe; but my false sense, which is mass sense or mass mesmerism, makes my individual universe the universe of all. We read in First Corinthians, "There hath no temptation taken you but such as is common to man." Likewise, there is no temptation that is common to mass sense or mass mesmerism that is not common to me. The good or evil of my individual universe is always impersonal. It is never my good or my evil, but the good of my world is the universal impersonal good that is God; and the evil of my world is the claim of universal false sense or mass mesmerism or mental malpractice which is common to all in varying degrees.

All error must be handled as impersonal, as false sense, as mental malpractice. If we hear of theft or murder, if we sense disease or disaster, if we sense limited health or limited success, we are not conscious of these until they appear in our consciousness; but they existed in belief as false or mass mesmerism or mental malpractice, else they could not have appeared as our sense world.

To myself, I am not the murderer or the thief or the sick man or the disaster, the limited health or the limited success. Yet I sense these experiences in belief, and whatever I sense in my world as evil is the one universal claim of false sense or mass mesmerism or mental malpractice appearing at the point of my individual consciousness and at no place else. And until I awaken to the spiritual fact of the one Mind as revealed in Christian Science, my universe will continue more or less to be a universe of false sense or mass mesmerism or mental malpractice. I am as much the murderer as he, and he as much as I, while I allow this false sense or mass mesmerism or mental malpractice to be something in my consciousness instead of nothing or nobody.

In the proportion that I make a reality of false sense or mass mesmerism or mental malpractice, I perpetuate my present sense-world as such. But when I return to "my Father's house" or true consciousness, I individualize my world in the ratio of my understanding of Truth. So long as I sense error of any kind it must be handled as impersonal, as false sense, as mass mesmerism, as mental malpractice, as ignorance of God, as nothing claiming to be something or somebody, or claiming to be my individual consciousness or my world. Because there is no evil, it is impossible for me to experience it, even in belief; I can only sense it in belief. In fact, I am always functioning as Mind, and I am experiencing only the good that Mind is being.

Individual and Universal Malpractice Healed

At this stage of spiritual discernment we cannot rest on the assumption that our apparent unconsciousness of error protects us from error; neither can we rest from our vigilance because the error appears to belong to someone else. Where an error appears in our world it is mental malpractice being uncovered as our conscious or unconscious thought; it is a demand upon us to heal ourselves only, and we do this at our individual point of consciousness.

The same unlovely traits of character and disposition, the same calamities and tragedies, the same limitations which have been in the world down through the ages, are our present world today. And they will continue to be our world, until we learn that the universal false beliefs or mass mesmerism or mental malpractice claiming to be our individual false consciousness, are impersonal, and can be overcome. We reform our world only as we reform ourselves. We change our false sense of things only as we perceive and understand the allness of God, good.

All false sense, war, lack, famine, hate — all of which are the phenomena of our ignorance of God and are mental malpractice — is met only at the point of our own individual consciousness. This is the only place it can be met, because it is the only place where it is going on so far as we are concerned. When we learn that Truth is uncovering the conscious and unconscious beliefs which claim to be our world, we will not look outside our own consciousness for the healing of murderers and thieves, lack and war, earthquakes and floods, which seem to go on as our world. There is in reality no wrong doer, no wrong doing, no sick man, no lack, no war, no floods, even in belief. I sense these things in belief because I individually am ignorant of the truth about these things; and it is my ignorance that causes actualities which are ever present to be seen in reversion or as "a bland denial of Truth."

All things of which we are conscious, even though appearing as the experience of someone else, are as much our experience as theirs and as little their experience as ours, and must be handled this way. When we clearly recognize that "what thou seest that thou beest," this fact will heal all criticism, all condemnation and self-righteousness that we may be harboring in thought. Since everything is transpiring as consciousness, then all false sense or mental malpractice is at the point of our own consciousness.

Malpractice, the Belief in More than One Mind

Malpractice is purely wrong practice. Since Christian Science is the Science of one Mind, then malpractice is the acceptance of the suggestion or the belief of two minds, which results in the belief of a matter body and a matter universe. This is the malpractice or wrong practice which is common to all. It is not the suggestion or the belief that is the malpractice, but we malpractice when we acquiesce to the suggestion or the belief of two minds. All crime, evil, lack, sickness and death exist as a state of consciousness only. These are active in our individual experience as false sense or mental malpractice, and appear in our consciousness because of our ignorance of only one Mind.

There is nothing external to our consciousness. If we seem to be ill, or seem to lack, or hate, it is because we have consented consciously or unconsciously to the suggestion that we have a mind apart from God. It is purely a belief of two minds. We may not have consciously thought disease or consciously accepted other beliefs that go with a mortal sense of existence; but if we do not consciously, through accurate scientific thinking, assume the attitude of one omnipresent, omnipotent Mind, we are not a law to our experience, and anything which mortal mind believes may claim to be our belief.

There is no outside world. Everything which we experience is in consciousness and exists to us according to our sense of the truth of it. Since our understanding of God is man and is our world, then if our understanding of God is limited or imperfect, we will experience a limited or imperfect man or world. The evil-doer that we seem to see outside of us is no more an evil-doer than we are when we consent to or recognize the evil as evil-doer, instead of recognizing the evil as nobody and nothing.

The only way to handle malpractice effectually is not to malpractice. We should never personalize evil, because evil is never a person, but is a lie about Truth. It is our ignorance of this ever-present Truth that is the malpractice. If Christ, Truth, is not present as our consciousness, then the lie or ignorance is present. There is no one to blame for our troubles; there is no enemy nor so-called organized evil. We need blame only our own ignorance or our own limited understanding of the one Mind, which is eternally omnipresent and omnipotent.

We are either acknowledging God, good, in all our ways, or we are consenting to or unconsciously accepting the prevailing beliefs of our world. When we say to ourselves, "Oh Lord, how long?" the answer comes back, "Just as long as you deny my omnipresence." To whine or complain as if something or somebody were doing something to us, unbidden or unknown to us, only adds to the confusion, for we are merely the victims of our own ignorant and limited sense of God.

There is a tendency among Christian Scientists to look upon the one Mind as a lovely ideal to be attained at some future time, and then talk and act as if another mind is also going on. There is a tendency to hold to the belief or suggestion of two minds. We must be alert to this.

Mortal mind or mental malpractice invariably claims to have a channel or medium — always someone thinking wrongly. But when we reject the suggestion that mortal mind is an entity or a mind, we also reject the channel or the personal medium. One of the errors of our movement is the belief that somebody is malpracticing. If we accept this suggestion we unwittingly become a malpractitioner, because we are believing in two minds, and this is "a bland denial of Truth."

Malpractice is not a reality; it is always a belief; and since there are no beliefs in infinity, and infinity is All, we can deal with malpractice as belief only. If someone is malpractising me, he is malpracticing himself, because he is malpractising his own belief. What difference does it make if ten thousand so-called people are saying two and two are five? This does not change the fact that two and two are four. And if many people work erroneously, what of it? They cannot harm or change anything. Why? Because they can never get their thought beyond themselves — beyond their own beliefs. In *Science and Health* Mrs. Eddy writes, "Evil thoughts, lusts, and malicious purposes cannot go forth, like wandering pollen, from one human mind to another, finding unsuspected lodgement, if virtue and truth build a strong defence."

There is only one Mind and that Mind is the one law-maker. There are therefore no malpractitioners who are making laws that can affect us. And since there is only one Mind, there are no malpractitioners, because there are not many minds. We never need to fear the malpractitioner, because he is merely a false belief about individual man. It is a great mistake to cause people to fear malpractice. Since our belief in malpractice and a malpractitioner necessarily exposes our own ignorance of God, the less said the better it will be for us and others.

Someone may ask, Shall we take cognizance of the claim of malpractice or just ignore it? There is a vast difference between our taking cognizance of a claim and ignoring a claim. When we scientifically cognize the claim of malpractice as a belief or false sense only, this destroys the claim of malpractice. We shall always keep on top of the situation if we realize that the claim of malpractice is nothing and nobody; therefore we do not have to resist it.

No matter what the claim appears to be, it should be recognized basically as fear. If we fear evil of any nature, then we are believing in it. The great thing is to be unafraid. The only Mind there is, is not afraid, and there is no other mind to be a channel for fear. We should deal with malpractice with the confidence that there is only one Mind, and this confidence is Immanuel or Mind with us. That which handles all malpractice is the fact that infinity is ever expressing itself, and that which represents infinity is man, and man is always in accord with infinity.

5. INFINITE IDEAS — HUMAN SUPPLY

Students, we all have a sense of limitation because as yet we have a limited sense of infinite good. We all, in some degree, have difficulty in demonstrating supply — in multiplying or increasing our good. There is a reason for this, and the reason is that we have not sufficiently learned how to translate our sense of things from a material to a spiritual basis. Yet Mrs. Eddy tells us in *Miscellaneous Writings* that "Science, understood, translates matter into Mind." Matter translated back into its original is Mind.

More or less, our sense has been that all things are external and apart from us, and that we must somehow attain them in order to have them. Also our sense of things, especially inanimate things, has been a finite and material sense. But now, in this new cycle of truer enlarged thinking, we are awakening to the necessity of evaluating all things, both animate and inanimate, as being spiritual ideas. After the experience of the past few years, we all see the necessity of basing our sense of things on a spiritual foundation in order that we may understand and demonstrate that all things which constitute our present consciousness are spiritual ideas, and are therefore ever-present, infinite and unfailing.

The student of Christian Science deals easily with many problems; but when it comes to the question of supply, there seems to be less of a basic, definite understanding, less of scientific thinking, and more of mass mesmerism and superstition than accompanies any other so-called problem. And while our sense of supply affects our human experience more keenly than any other problem, we continue in some degree to "walk . . . *into* or *with*, the currents of matter, or mortal mind" on this most important subject.

There is much mass mesmerism connected with the problem of supply which we, as students, cannot afford to ignore. Because of our ignorance of the realities of existence, there is the almost universal mesmerism which causes us to believe, consciously or unconsciously, that God or Mind has little to do with our supply. There is the belief that our supply is almost entirely in the hands of other persons and little in our own hands or the hands of God. There is the belief that our position, our income, our employment, are disconnected from us and are at the mercy of others, and that we ourselves have little power over these things. It is almost a prevailing belief that our business is dependent upon the activities of other persons, upon the activities of our government, or of nations, or of international conditions, and is entirely out of God's hands.

However, in the proportion that we understand the co-ordination of all things, the reciprocal law of divine being, and our inseparable oneness with God, our own Mind, we will free ourselves from all this mass mesmerism. Mind is unifying, co-operative and reciprocal, because one Mind only is unfolding itself out into indivisible infinity. Everything in the universe belongs to God, to Mind; everything is in His hands; everything of which we are conscious has its being, its substance and all its activities in the one divine Principle. Likewise everything in the universe belongs to us. Each one of us is an individual expression of infinity, and consequently each one of us possesses all the glories of heaven and earth.

When once we understand that it is our ignorance of God and man as one being that causes the false sense which seems to hide our real heritage, we will reject this false sense, and be more alert in basing our thinking on the spiritual sense of God and man. There is no separation between God and man, between Principle and idea, between infinity and its expression. Then, students, since God and man are one being, there can be no such thing as a claim of poverty and lack; and the *fear* of poverty and lack is all there is to the claim.

We, as Christian Scientists, should never ignore the claim of lack of any nature, neither should we ignore the fear of it; but we should understand the absolute nothingness of the claim, and have confidence in the certainty and permanency of God and man as one being. The claim of an insufficient income, so long associated with many of us, should be disposed of, at least in a measure, and we should come naturally and consciously into infinite possessions. The fact that we identify all that God is, is true now, and is demonstrated in the measure that we actually understand and individualize this fact.

Consciousness Outpictured as Tangible Ideas

Perhaps the most aggressive mass mesmerism is that we can think about a thing and still not consciously have it; that we can think about health and wealth and still not consciously experience them in our daily living. Nevertheless, the fact that we think about health and wealth, is the fact that they already are in our individual consciousness as a conscious experience. What we call our thinking about health and wealth is the presence of health and wealth in our consciousness.

The student of Christian Science should be keenly alert and individualize the fact that things exist only because they have been thought or conceived by God, his Mind, and therefore constitute his own individual consciousness. God, or Mind, is ever conscious, and everything in the universe has been evolved by this conscious Mind as thought or infinite ideas, and these still appear humanly as material things. It is most important to understand that the universe of so-called material things is the universe of thoughts or ideas. God, or conscious Mind, is in manifestation as an infinity of ideas, and this infinity of ideas constitutes consciousness or intelligence, or individual man. In Christian Science we do not think of ourselves or individual man as personal or corporeal or material, but we think of ourselves as man or consciousness. We think of ourselves as an infinite compound of all the ideas that identify God, or Mind, and constitute our consciousness.

We, as Christian Scientists, often fail to evaluate correctly the things of which we are conscious. We should evaluate everything of which we are conscious, no matter how it may appear to us humanly, as being one with God and therefore infinite and spiritual. All is infinite Mind infinitely manifested, from a world to a potato patch, from a blade of grass to a star, from a pin to a palace. Everything of which we are conscious makes up our compound idea of ourselves; everything is inseparable from God or Mind; everything is what Mind is consciously being, and is infinite and spiritual; everything is the manifestation of Mind and is spiritual man himself, no matter what false sense says about it.

Everything of which we are conscious is a conscious idea. It is alive; it is living. There is no such thing as an unconscious or inanimate idea. Every idea manifests consciousness. By virtue of the fact that all things constitute consciousness, every idea or every thing is divinely conscious. A stone — an idea — does not think, (only God or Mind thinks), yet a stone is a conscious idea, for it is something in consciousness. What a stone or money really is, as idea, may not be fully revealed to us as yet; but we know they are ideas in consciousness, and can, therefore, be demonstrated by us.

In universal belief the things of which we are conscious are divided into opposing groups — the animate and the inanimate, the spiritual and the material, the divine and the human. But in Christian Science we learn that these opposites are not two, but one; that the inanimate is only a false sense of the animate; that matter is but a false concept of spiritual ideas; and that the divine idea appears as the human — all because of our ignorance of God and man as one being.

In Christian Science, we learn that everything which appears to us humanly can be demonstrated to be a divine idea. Everything which appears as a material object or an object of sense is a divine idea; and because it is divine and infinite, we each of us possess it. In the Gospel story, even the fish included the tax money. Everything that appears as an inanimate object, from a pin to a palace, is in reality an infinite idea. Everything of which we are conscious exists in consciousness; and it makes no difference how

43

infinitesimal it seems to be, or how material it seems to be to the human sense, it is idea and is infinite and divine.

It may appear to us that the thing we call animate in nature, is easier to understand as idea than the thing we call inanimate. For example, a horse in belief is a living animate creature; but in reality all there is to a horse is a divine idea. In belief the horse, because of its apparent life, appears different from a table or a chair or money or a loaf of bread, which we call inanimate objects with no apparent life. Nevertheless in reality the table, the chair, the money and the loaf of bread, are living conscious ideas which are imperfectly seen by us. Everything we believe to be inanimate, when dissociated from matter and understood as divine consciousness, will lose the limitations of matter and be seen in its true depict.

The Example of Loaves and Fishes

With five thousand people to be fed, the disciples brought to Jesus five loaves and two fishes as representing all the food available. Five loaves and two fishes was the disciples' limited sense of the availability of food, but this was not the vision of Jesus. Jesus knew loaf and fish were infinite, divine ideas infinitely expressed, and he knew that each one of the multitude — being the conscious infinite identity of the one Mind — included in his consciousness all that Mind included. Therefore, each one of the multitude included loaf and fish. But the multitude were ignorant of their oneness with God, or Mind. They were unaware that they identified infinite plenty. To them loaf and fish were separate from their consciousness, and they thought they had to attain them in order to have them. To the multitude the supply was limited, and to their false sense it was material.

The vision of Jesus, however, was above the human sense, or the ignorant limited sense of food as material. The very food which the disciples and the multitude considered as material and limited, Jesus understood as divine and infinite. Jesus interpreted food from a spiritual basis, and his true discernment of divine substance resulted in the inexhaustible and illimitable supply of thought and things, and appeared humanly to the disciples and to the multitude as loaves and fishes in abundance.

Jesus saw in the loaves and fishes his own true concept of food. To Jesus, food was a divine idea identifying infinite spiritual substance, and could be increased or multiplied wherever he was according to the amount he needed, even though the place was a desert and the necessity was food for five thousand. Jesus saw food as a spiritual idea — universal, omnipresent, and at hand. But the multitude, whose concept of food was still limited and material, no doubt saw in this spiritual expression of infinite good only their old familiar so-called loaves and fishes. To the materialist, all things are material. To the spiritually minded, all things are in and of Spirit. And, students, if things appear to us, individually, as material and limited, the trouble is not with the things, but with the lens through which we see them.

Objects of Sense Exchanged for Ideas

In divine Science everything that appears humanly is a divine idea. That which appears to us humanly as a material object is, in reality, a divine idea. Objects of sense are really ideas of Soul. An idea of Soul, seen through the lens of material sense, may appear as a material object or a material thing, but there is only one thing present, and this is the idea of Soul. Right where the finite material object of sense seems to be, there the right idea is — in my mind or consciousness.

Objects of sense do not exist in reality; they exist as false appearance only. Therefore, objects of sense have neither place nor limitation. What appears to my consciousness as material limited things, are merely my human sense of divine ideas. Man, tree and flower appear to die, but they never do die because they are divine ideas — one with God, immortal Life. Man, tree and flower, according to material sense, are the human sense of divine immortal substance. Ideas are never temporal things — there are no temporal things. The so-called temporal things are but the false interpretations of eternal things. All things are one with God and are immortal.

Let us remember that every divine idea we entertain in consciousness, is the presence of God or Mind unfolding as our consciousness; it is present as our Mind and appearing as power, presence, law, achievement and intelligence in the measure of our understanding.

Money, a house, a table, or an automobile exist as ideas only, but to our human concept they are objects of sense with measurements and limitations and material accompaniments. They are the human concepts of divine ideas, and we are told in our textbook that we must replace human concepts with divine ideas, or, we must exchange the objects of sense for the ideas of Soul. The words *replace* and *exchange* might be very misleading if we think there are two entities — one to be replaced or exchanged for the other. We as students must clearly understand that what appears as an object of sense is present right here and now as a spiritual idea, and has the presence, form, color, substance and tangibility of Spirit.

A divine idea is immortal and exists at hand in its reality. This is why we can always demonstrate it. Everything which we wish to demonstrate already exists. Every attribute and quality of the thing to be demonstrated already exists. If things or certain attributes or qualities seem to be absent or limited, it is because of our limited sense of divine, infinite substance, God. Money, a house, an automobile, a table, a friend, and all other things which appear to meet the need of humanity today, are only a material limited sense of what is present as ideas of completeness, wholeness, satisfaction, and ease — ideas which are contributive to a perfect state of being.

We need to understand that all these things which appear to meet our human needs are Mind, God, manifested as ideas, and are not the material things they appear to be. When we understand them as ideas, they will always bless us, always add to our comfort and happiness and well-being, and always satisfy us. Every idea of God's creation is ours and constitutes our consciousness, not sometime, but now; and our consciousness is even now conscious of itself as infinite good.

Students, it is right and natural that we should have an enlarged sense of this infinite good in our present state of consciousness. If we could free ourselves from the false education of the senses and accept our birthright as the sons of God, then there would appear this conscious continuity of all good, experienced as ascending states of consciousness, until all so-called material objects would be seen in their divine character.

The textbook tells us, "Understanding . . . is the reality of all things brought to light." Hence, there is the great need to understand the certainty and permanency and eternality of all that we are conscious of humanly. This understanding is a protection for those of us who seem to have little, as well as for those who have much; for it is only as we understand that all things of which we are conscious are divine ideas, that we can prove their permanency and their ever-present availability.

6. WHAT IS CHRISTIAN SCIENCE HEALING?

Several years ago while visiting with the Christian Science teacher Bicknell Young, he said to me, "You must learn to read *Science and Health* correctly in order to do good healing work." And, students, if we as Christian Scientists understood the truths in our textbook in the light of Mrs. Eddy's understanding, we would derive far greater benefits from our practice of Christian Science.

There are two fundamental points in our healing work which should be clarified. The first is that our thought should be especially clear as to the true meaning of healing. Healing is not healing in the usual sense of restoring something, but healing is a process of thinking which reveals that which is already whole and perfect. We might say to a patient, "I cannot heal you — that is restore you — but I can reveal to you yourself as you already are."

The second fundamental point in our healing work is a true evaluation of the claims of mortal mind. All the claims of mortal mind — such as fear, doubt, worry, hate, anger, lack, or disease — are sin. Sin as used in our textbook, is a name which designates that which is never active, never conscious, never present, never existent. All sin is ignorance of Truth. All sin is the claim that there can be the absence of Mind or the absence of understanding.

In our practice work we do not heal — that is restore these claims of evil to good; neither do we destroy these claims. But through the analysis of the evil and through reason and logic as set forth for us in our textbook, we find that all sin or evil is neither cause nor effect, and is as powerless to harm us as is our ignorance of music or mathematics.

In our textbook, Mrs. Eddy did not set out the claims of mortal mind to show us how to heal or destroy them, but through her analysis of the claims and through reason, revelation, and logic, she reduced the claims of mortal mind to their native nothingness. In other words she took off the chariot wheels of the Egyptians for us. Mrs. Eddy saw the importance of evaluating all claims of mortal mind, not as something to be healed or destroyed, but to be understood as nothing.

The world in general and many Christian Scientists, are of the opinion that the practice of Christian Science is for the express purpose of healing — that is, restoring — the diseased body and demonstrating supply. But the fact is that healing as revealed by Christian Science has little to do with a diseased body or with lack. Christian Science is the Science of one infinite Mind — a Mind that includes no evil. Christian Science teaches that the claims of so-called mortal mind are reduced to their nothingness and self-destroyed through analysis, reason, revelation, and logic, which we gain through a deep and intensive study of our textbook.

In *Rudimental Divine Science*, Mrs. Eddy says, "Healing physical sickness is the smallest part of Christian Science. It is only the bugle-call to thought and action, in the higher range of infinite goodness. The emphatic purpose of Christian Science is the healing of sin." But the healing of sin does not mean that the claim of sin exists as a fact. Mrs. Eddy, through her analysis of the claim of sin, reduced this claim to its nothingness, just as she did the claim of sickness.

The Requirements of Christian Science Healing

Often in our healing work, we fail to fulfill the requirements of Christian Science — the Science of Mind. In our treatments — that is, in the use of the affirmations of truth and the denials of error, we very often predicate our affirmations and denials on the assumption that there is disease to be eradicated. And when we do this, we let our treatment fall to the plane of *materia medica*, which always considers disease as an entity or condition to be disposed of. Also when we use a treatment to eradicate sin or evil, we are placing Christian Science treatment on the same plane as scholastic theology, which considers sin and evil as entities — as something to be disposed of, or eradicated from the minds of mortals.

The difficulty is that we fail to keep our treatment on the plane of divine Mind, where thought operates as omnipresence. So often when arguing, we get away from the standpoint of divine Mind. But to keep our treatment scientific, we must always argue from the standpoint of the omnipresence and omniscience of God. In the textbook Mrs. Eddy says, "Remember that the letter and mental argument are only human auxiliaries to aid in bringing thought into accord with the spirit of Truth and Love, which heals the sick and the sinner."

It is the Christ — the living, conscious, irresistible understanding or true consciousness — which heals, and heals by its all-presence. It is not because of us or because of the human arguments that we employ, that the healing takes place; but it is the Christ, the Truth within, that does the healing.

In our healing, it does seem that a practitioner does something for someone else; but as practitioners, we should always bear in mind that someone else is not someone else to God. We, as practitioners, realize that the one who appears to be a patient is now the son of God. What appears as a patient is the appearing of man — the coincidence of the human and the divine. In belief, the dream and the dreamer are one. The practitioner is part of the dream; but when we, as practitioners, rise out of the dream into true consciousness, we no longer see a patient as a patient, but we see "the perfect man." The less we feel that we have a patient, the fewer failures we shall have in our practice work. A patient is always the divine Mind unfolding, and there is no place where divine Mind is not expressing Himself as perfect man. There is no patient to the I AM THAT I AM.

The Healing Standpoint

What is the process of healing? Healing is the increasing awareness of perfection, rather than the eradication of disease. We should recognize that the healing process takes place coincidentally with our individual spiritual unfoldment.

A faithful student of Christian Science for many years found herself in bondage to what is called a fibroid tumor. For years the growth grew larger; and although she had had several practitioners, the condition grew worse instead of better. She was led to ask another consecrated practitioner for help. This practitioner said to the afflicted woman, "Are you looking for ease in matter? Are you looking for disease to be removed or eradicated from your body, or are you seeking to love God, Truth, with your whole heart, and praying for the Mind of Christ?" The practitioner also said, "All that needs to be removed or dissolved, is your belief that you are a selfhood apart from God, constituted of self-will, self-justification, and self-love; and this adamant of error — this belief of two minds — can only be removed or dissolved with the universal solvent of Love." Then she turned to *Science and Health* where Mrs. Eddy asks the question, "Dost thou 'love the Lord thy God, with all thy heart, and with all thy soul, and with all thy mind'?"

The student glimpsed that as this love for the one God became supreme in her affections, it would displace or remove properly — first mentally, then physically — whatever was unlovely or unlike the Christ in her consciousness. For several weeks she spent every spare minute in the prayerful study of the Bible and our Leader's writings, and she began to have such mental freedom that she could say, "Even if there does seem to be a tumor attached to me, I am knowing and loving the one God supremely."

Finally the fear of the growth began to disappear. Then came the joyous realization that since God is all Life, all substance, and all intelligence, surely matter could not make her believe that it was a living, intelligent, growing entity. A few days after this clear view of God's allness, she saw the result of correct thinking. The tumor passed away painlessly and with no after-effects. This student had found the process for the healing of all disease — the spiritualization of thought. She learned through this experience, as we all have to learn, that we have to earn our understanding of God, just as we have to earn our understanding of mathematics or music.

Healing does not mean the eradication of disease. If we think that we find health only as we eradicate disease, we perpetuate the disease. A knowledge of the one God as our health is what banishes disease permanently. When the truth was revealed to us through Christian Science that man is as perfect as God is perfect, there was also revealed to us the fact that spiritual unfoldment is the healing process.

Through the Science of healing, it is made evident that everything that exists is perfect now. We can all be healed because we are whole now. If we heal a case of so-called heart trouble, it is because the only heart there is needs no healing. The heart we now have indicates a divine fact imperfectly conceived. What appears to us as a material heart is a divine idea now, and it is perfect now. As this understanding is accepted in consciousness it excludes the need of healing so-called heart trouble. Spirit alone constitutes being. Spirit is substance — infinite substance. Then disease is no part of existence. This is a scientific fact, and we can prove it through the Science of healing.

Dr. Mayo says, "Disease is rebellion against fundamental law and order. Every abnormal growth is rebellion in a single cell which then multiplies." From this statement, Dr. Mayo thinks, and the world in general thinks, that disease has a mental cause. There is also the popular belief that Christian Science teaches that the human mind is the cause of all disease and affects the material body for good or ill. All these beliefs, which are the sins of the world, are, of course, untrue. And in contradistinction to these beliefs, Christian Science teaches the allness of the one Mind.

There is the prevalent belief that fear and anger disturb digestion; that hate is a deadly poison; that thought can generate lesions. All this has been mistakenly said to agree with the teachings of Christian Science, but such beliefs are sin and are untrue. The textbook tells us, "Such theories have no relationship to Christian Science, which rests on the conception of God as the only Life, substance, and intelligence, and excludes the human mind as a spiritual factor in the healing work."

If we accept the belief that all sin, disease, tragedies and calamities are caused by rebellion, hate, resentment, worry, doubt and fear, then we must accept the belief of a material creation governed by a mind capable of evil thinking. But this is all contrary to the teachings of Christian Science. Emotional disturbances such as rebellion, resistance, worry, hate, or fear have no power in and of themselves, and cannot, therefore, cause derangements or disease. Emotionalism belongs to mortal mind which, Mrs. Eddy teaches, is never substance, but is illusion, is ignorance only, is the false representation of man.

It is most necessary to study our textbook with an understanding mind. On page 411 we read, "The procuring cause and foundation of all sickness is fear, ignorance, or sin." To the unenlightened thought, this might imply that mortal mind does cause disease. But this reference from our textbook is not a statement of fact, but is the analysis of sickness as mental and not physical. On page 419 we find the opposite statement. "Neither disease itself, sin, nor fear has the power to cause disease or a relapse." And on page 415 we read, "Immortal Mind is the only cause; therefore disease is neither a cause nor an effect."

Evils must be disposed of scientifically. We do not experience sin and disease; we sense them in belief — the same as we sensed a green horse because of green glasses. Likewise, we see perfect creation — man and the universe — as material, deformed, diseased, insufficient, or dead, because we see through the lens of material sense. The imperfections we sense are no more conditions to be eradicated or removed from perfect creation, than greenness was a condition to be eradicated or removed from the white horse. Unless we perceive that creation is perfect and spiritual now, we "have no Principle to demonstrate and no rule for its demonstration."

Disease Not Located in the Body or the Human Mind

In our healing work, it is most necessary to understand that we never locate disease in the body. The body has absolutely nothing to do with the experience called disease. A student in a distant city told her practitioner that she had had liver trouble for thirty-five years. The practitioner insisted that she must not locate the trouble in her body. This student sent a special delivery letter to me, asking if she was wrong in locating liver trouble in the liver.

I replied emphatically that she was wrong in locating disease in her body; that if she had kept the trouble in her liver for thirty-five years, and continued to do so, she would likely keep it there thirty-five years longer; she could not do anything to it as long as it was in her body. I told her that Christian Science teaches us that all disease is an image in mortal thought, and then gave her the following references:

"Too soon we cannot turn from disease in the body to find disease in the mortal mind, and its cure, in working for God." (*Miscellaneous Writings*) "Whatever is cherished in mortal mind as the physical condition is imaged forth on the body." (*Science and Health*) "So-called disease is a sensation of mind, not of matter." (*Miscellany*)

Then I tried to show her that after transposing the trouble from her body to her mind, if she left it in her mind as mental, she would be little better off than before. But if she clearly understood that disease was not a condition in her body, but was simply an image of mortal thought, then she had dominion over it. I told her that she was greater than her thoughts and feelings, and could therefore deal with the sense of disease at the point of her own belief in it. Only at this mental point could she actually contact what she called liver trouble and what comprised that sense.

Human goodness does not work out the problem of being. We must be scientific Christians. To accept Christianity without its

Science is to accept scholastic theology, which is a belief in two minds. Christian Science is the Science of one Mind, and humanity's only sin is believing in and practicing from the standpoint of two minds.

Mrs. Eddy clearly states the way of deliverance for all mankind in the textbook when she says, "There is but one way to heaven, harmony, and Christ in divine Science shows us this way. It is to know no other reality — to have no other consciousness of life — than good, God and His reflection, and to rise superior to the so-called pain and pleasure of the senses."

GOD, MIND, CONSCIOUSNESS
Association Address of 1940

GOD, MIND, CONSCIOUSNESS
Association Address of 1940

by

Martha Wilcox

Dear Students: As in other years, we assemble here for the purpose of gaining an enlarged understanding of the power and presence of God. Untold blessings, which we all desire, are not the result of a meager understanding, but untold blessings are the natural outcome of an enlarged understanding of God and His perfect creation.

Indeed, an altitude of understanding is the door to infinite good. The measure of our understanding of God and man and the universe, is the measure of our condition of existence. If our understanding is limited, we are deprived of much of ourselves; but if our understanding is infinite, this infinite understanding includes the all of ourselves.

We, as students of Christian Science, understand much about God and the real man and the real universe. We are all trying to demonstrate a greater understanding; and what we accomplish through our degree of understanding is far greater than what is accomplished by any other method.

Today, it is quite fitting to remind ourselves that what we understand of God and Christian Science is due to Mrs. Eddy's revelation. There had to be a discoverer to reach out and beyond other methods; and it was our beloved Mrs. Eddy who looked beyond the orthodox and scientific theories of her age, and perceived the meaning and the character of the Word of God; and from her true perception of the Word of God she gave us divine Science.

There were many philosophies and theories in Mrs. Eddy's day. The natural scientists were all diligently striving to find the cause of all existing things, but they were not looking in the right direction. It was impossible to find the cause of creation without the correct perception of the Word of God, and His true character; and these natural scientists failed to discern the fact that creation, in order to be active and operative, must have a divine cause. It remained for Mrs. Eddy to discern this divine cause, and so become the Discoverer and Founder of Christian Science.

1. GOD, MIND, CONSCIOUSNESS

In order that our understanding of the meaning and character of the word *God* may be further enlarged, let us consider the three words which comprise our first subject — the words God, Mind and consciousness. These three words signify that which is primal.

The word primal means that which is first — that upon which everything depends for its substance and existence. Since God, Mind, or consciousness is primal, then everything and every individual depends upon God, Mind, or consciousness for their substance and existence. The correct understanding of these three words in the mind of the student establishes a practical working basis in the practice of Christian Science.

The word God signifies a state or mode of active, conscious Truth or good. When we say the word God, there should be present as our consciousness a state of active, conscious Truth or good. We should understand that whatever degree of Truth, or good, is present in our consciousness — even though it appears humanly or materially because seen through the lens of material sense — it is Truth or good.

Mrs. Eddy uses the word Mind for God in Christian Science, in contradistinction to the meaning of the word God as formerly used by orthodox theology. The word Mind for God not only

60

gave an entirely new meaning to God, but it also gave an entirely new meaning to the word mind. It took away the limited meaning of the word mind.

As we begin to understand that the word God means limitless Mind, and as we understand that the Mind we now have, is limitless God, then our mind begins to yield up its supposed limitation along all lines. We begin to yield up the universal belief that our mind is formed in the brain and operates as human opinions; we yield up the belief that Mind is confined in matter, or that it could be what is called mortal mind. Since we prove through Christian Science that Mind is God, and that God is Mind, we can also prove that Mind is without limitations of power or space or time, and is limitless intelligence; and what we humanly conceive of as mind, we now find to be limitless in its nature without beginning of years or end of days.

The one Mind is primal. We, as students, should give the word Mind much consideration. We should think about Mind, because the so-called human mind that we have, here and now, is God — the divine Mind. It only seems to be human because imperfectly known. The Mind we now have is the only God we shall ever have; therefore let us give to our Mind the best and highest meaning we can, and permit that meaning to expand and expand and expand.

We should not talk of mortal mind as though it were Mind, as though it were actively doing something or thinking something. If we do, it gives the impression that there are two minds — one active as good, and one active as evil. So-called mortal mind, or carnal mind, or personal mind, is not mind at all — it does not exist or operate. It is the supposed absence of the one Mind, or consciousness of Spirit; it is the name for our ignorance of God and man, as they are in reality.

We should never identify ourselves with mortal mind; if we do, we are identifying ourselves as mortal. We should always identify ourselves as immortal. It means much to know that our Mind is

God — is good, is ever active, is ever kind, is ever joyful, is ever pure, is ever available through Christian Science. Christian Science is the Science of divine Mind, and the Science of divine Mind is ever operative as law in our behalf. To understand these truths, is to do much for ourselves and for mankind.

The word God not only signifies the one Mind, but it also signifies the one consciousness. God, Mind, consciousness, is not three separate entities, or three different modes of existence, but is one successive, fuller unfoldment of the one and only cause.

The use of the word Mind for God brought the true character of God so close to us that we have come to accept God as being Mind, as being our Mind. The use of the word consciousness for God, when defined spiritually and scientifically, has given us a full conception of ourselves as we are in Truth. And with the realization that we are a mode of conscious existence, we have come to accept God as being consciousness — as being our consciousness.

In all our mental work for ourselves and for others, it is most necessary to understand that God, Mind, consciousness, is a conscious mode of existence identified as man. Our conscious existence is not conscious of something apart or external to itself, but consciousness is all-inclusive. Our mode of consciousness (conscious existence) is constituted of all existing things — man and the universe.

Man, the Identity of Consciousness

In *Unity of Good*, Mrs. Eddy wonderfully expresses the fact that God, or Mind, is an infinite mode of consciousness. She says: "All consciousness [meaning wherever there is consciousness] is Mind; and Mind is God — an infinite, and not a finite consciousness." Consciousness is God, or Mind, present and operative as the one self-conscious existence. We call this infinite mode of conscious existence, human consciousness, but this is because we see through the lens of finite material sense. Mrs. Eddy continues: "This consciousness is reflected in individual consciousness, or man, whose source is infinite Mind. There is no really finite mind, no finite consciousness." It is a wonderful thing to have revealed to us that individual consciousness, or individual man, is the reflection or conscious identity of the one all-inclusive consciousness.

To what extent are we consciously identifying with this all-inclusive consciousness? To what extent do we reflect, or exhibit to the world, our mode of pure consciousness? In our daily so-called human life are we definitely aware that the consciousness we have here and now, is the conscious identity of the consciousness of infinite good, or do we still dwell in the false sense that our consciousness is finite and personal?

Consciousness is never limited nor personal. A person does not include consciousness. Consciousness itself is all-inclusive and reflects this all-inclusiveness as man. God, or consciousness, could not include a personal sense of individual man; therefore, a person is never the evidence of Mind or consciousness, but always a false sense of individual man. The word person has a finite meaning, while the word God, or Mind, has an infinite meaning. Since the word God, or Mind, means consciousness, it therefore cannot mean a personal consciousness or person. There is no such thing as a personal consciousness. What appears to be a personal consciousness, is in reality an individual expression of the one infinite consciousness, although imperfectly known to us. Let us always give consciousness its true value regardless of appearance.

Consciousness has an idea of itself, or looks back upon itself. Consciousness can know only its own subjective state, and all it ever sees and knows is good and very good. Consciousness cannot know anything other than itself. It sees and knows only its own qualities. There is nothing that can produce consciousness, because consciousness itself is God. We can never go back further than our own consciousness, because there is nothing further back. Consciousness is. There is nothing to God and man but the one consciousness.

The showing forth of the identity of the one consciousness which is man, can show forth no inclination, no capacity, no cause or effect separate from the one consciousness. Man cannot think; that is, man cannot originate thought. Man is the thinking that Mind is doing. Therefore, since there is no mortality or imperfection in consciousness, there can be none in His conscious identity, or man.

The narrative of the three Hebrew boys shows clearly that consciousness includes no destructive flames. Then the individual consciousness of the three Hebrew boys, being the conscious identity of the one consciousness, could include no destructive flames; therefore they could not be burned. Their pure mode of consciousness enabled them to walk through the flames unharmed. The Hebrews had no sense of resistance to destructiveness of any kind; they were not conscious of the flames as destructive, therefore they had no resistance to them. Their identity of the one consciousness permitted them to come out of the furnace unharmed.

Four days after the decease of Lazarus, Jesus came to the tomb, having excluded from his own consciousness the belief of death, the belief of time, the belief of disintegration. Jesus knew that since such experiences were unknown to true consciousness, they were unknown likewise to Lazarus. Lazarus, being God's idea of Himself, or man, had never lived in matter or in a material body, and never died out of it. Jesus knew that there was nothing in the consciousness of Lazarus that could say, "I am dead." Lazarus was the conscious identity of the one infinite consciousness, therefore he came forth exhibiting this one consciousness and was seen to human comprehension as the normal state of a human being.

The God-consciousness was the consciousness that was Jesus, and was also the consciousness of Lazarus — the perfect man that Jesus saw. There never was a sinning mortal man, or a sick man, or a dead man in consciousness. God's conscious idea of Himself could not be mortal, sick or dead. Sin, sickness and death are impossible since they are not in consciousness, and we, like the Hebrew boys, should have no resistance to them. Jesus understood man to be an eternal living mode of consciousness, and he understood God and man to be one and the same conscious mode. Jesus was constantly aware of the oneness of God and man as consciousness.

God, Mind, consciousness, is the name given to the infinitude of self-conscious good, and because this good is self-conscious, there is the infinite idea of good, or man. Mrs. Eddy says in *Science and Health*, "Spirit is the only substance and consciousness recognized by divine Science," and, "Real consciousness is cognizant only of the things of God," She also says, "There is no other consciousness."

Immanence, a Quality of Consciousness

Year after year in our association meetings one dominant note has prevailed — the immanence of God, or the immanence of Mind, or the immanence of consciousness. And as we are emphasizing consciousness today, we shall endeavor to reveal the immeasurable value of the quality of immanence in consciousness. (Immanent: Remaining or operating within the subject considered; indwelling; inherent; subjective. Webster)

Immanence is a distinct quality of consciousness that must be discerned and understood and practiced by us in order to have results in the practice of Christian Science. Because of this characteristic of immanence, the one consciousness states and perpetually cognizes His own acts and His own being, and there is no other being.

Because of this quality of immanence we are proving through Christian Science that everything exists in infinity. Everything that has ever existed or will ever exist, was in the beginning inherent or indwelling within consciousness subjectively.

When we speak of man and the universe as subjective, we mean that the universe and man, as effect or manifestation, is one and the same with its cause, or that the universe and man is inherent or indwelling within its cause here and now. That is, when we see the universe and man, we see God, cause in effect, as expression.

Because of this quality of immanence, which means that everything known is subjective, we understand that consciousness cannot produce or be anything beyond Himself or apart from Himself. Therefore everything, regardless of appearance, is God, good, eternal, indestructible, whole — *now*.

All things, all conditions, all events, when correctly understood, are what consciousness is conscious of, as Himself; and whatever these things, conditions or events are in their conscious identity, individual consciousness or individual man is that. There is nothing outside or beside or unlike or other than the one conscious Mind. He is all-inclusive, and the universe and man are held within this one consciousness.

When we understand that the one infinite consciousness is forever disclosing Himself to Himself as what He is — and He is All — and what this All is in its conscious identity, we realize that that is individual consciousness or individual man. There is no one outside of or beside consciousness to whom consciousness could disclose Himself. We understand that what consciousness is or does, is done wholly within Himself, and is wholly of Himself, and is wholly Himself.

We, as students of Christian Science, should understand that immanence is the unfailing characteristic of consciousness, that holds all that consciousness is within itself, inherently and subjectively and forever.

Let us consider the quality in consciousness that we experience humanly as health. This quality of health dwells subjectively within its cause — God. Since health was in the beginning with consciousness, and remains forever in oneness and sameness with its original, conscious cause, then health cannot be impaired or lost or fail.

Since the quality of health in the one infinite consciousness cannot be impaired or lost or fail, because it is subjectively in consciousness, then the conscious identity of health — which is the individual's consciousness — cannot be impaired or lost or fail. The individual's consciousness of health is the showing forth of the conscious identity of the one consciousness.

Because of the quality of immanence, we have never been apart from or unlike our Maker. Our Maker, or true consciousness, has always held each one within Himself subjectively. Since this is true, were we ever born? Since we are a subjective state of our Maker, we were never subject to death. It is well that we understand these things.

Since man and the universe are within consciousness, subjectively, and are disclosed as His conscious presence and substance, can man or the universe be a medium for sin, disease or death? The qualities of sin, disease and death not being inherent in consciousness, and not being held subjectively within consciousness, cannot therefore exist in His conscious manifestation — man and the universe. Since cause or consciousness is not conscious of sin, disease or death, then man and the universe cannot be conscious of, subject to, or aware of these falsities.

Since everything that exists is indwelling, or is subjectively in its cause or consciousness, and is in oneness and sameness with its cause or consciousness, then where do fear and weariness and unhappiness and poverty and disease and dissatisfaction originate? Where do envy and hatred and jealousy originate? Where do the claims of influenza and high blood pressure originate? Where do fever and pain and inflammation begin? Where and how does a personality originate? How can a personality subject to birth, age and death fill space? How and where do evil and matter hold sway?

There is but one answer to these startling questions. Since these qualities are not inherent in, or held subjectively in God, Mind, consciousness — the only cause — they cannot be the experience of man and the universe. Therefore sin, disease and death never did originate, and they are unknown. They do not exist at all! As Christian Scientists, we should strive diligently to perceive and understand the immanence of consciousness, and we should keep on striving until consciously we approximate that state of consciousness wherein there is no imperfection at all.

Creation Subjective to the Creator

The word creator as generally used is often misleading. It usually implies that all existing things are apart and unlike their creator instead of being in oneness and sameness with Him. As generally used, creator implies that there was a time when things did not exist, and later a time when things were brought into existence. In fact, there never was a time when there was no creation, never a time when the creator was less than infinite, less than fully developed, less than complete, less than eternally finished. The one great creator — God, Mind, consciousness — has ever existed and ever expressed Himself in perfect harmony, as man and the universe.

Because the whole of creation exists subjectively, in the creator, the creator consciously guides, governs, protects, preserves, and sustains every existing thing. Every existing thing lives and moves and has being in Him subjectively.

Since God, Mind, consciousness, the creator of all things, is wholly and eternally good, then creation, being co-existent with and subjectively within the creator, must likewise be wholly and eternally good, without beginning and without end. So-called destructive beliefs could not possibly be within divine consciousness subjectively, which is wholly good and eternal. Therefore, such beliefs never had a beginning. They are unknown in consciousness and are not in His conscious identity — man.

Subjective and Objective Thinking

So-called human thoughts, when good and right, are the thought-forms or the so-called things of divine Mind — our Mind — although imperfectly known by us, and still seen objectively.

Humanly speaking, when our thinking is about things and about events and about conditions which seem apart from and external to us, this is called objective thinking.

But in subjective thinking, we understand that all thought-forms, events and conditions are held within their divine cause — our Mind — subjectively. We ourselves are the thought-forms, the events, the conditions as effect or manifestation, and they are good and eternally good. We should understand the great value in our practice work in keeping all our thinking subjective.

As yet, we still see things objectively before our mind — that is, we see them as apart and external to us. But through reason and revelation, we understand that these things are held in oneness within their cause. They were in the beginning with their cause, and are like their cause, and are governed and controlled by their cause. And we, as Christian Scientists, are to interpret all things from this viewpoint, and evaluate all things as subjective and not objective.

To Jesus everything was subjective — in and of the Father, Mind. To Jesus, everything, every event, every condition, everything that comprised Jesus as the conscious identity of Mind, was held subjectively in his own God-Mind. His own God-Mind was the cause of all these things, therefore they were externally like their cause — whole and complete and perfect.

Because of this quality of immanence in God, Mind, consciousness, we understand that every existing thing in the universe and in man, must be subjective — must be inherent or indwelling in consciousness, subjectively. Every condition, or event, or experience is mental — is divinely mental — and is subjective. And we are to understand these things as subjective or indwelling in consciousness, no matter what the false appearance may be.

God — our Mind, the only consciousness — is the Maker of all our thoughts, ideas and experiences, and they are subjective, even if they appear before the so-called human mind objectively. Everything is subjective and starts from within our own God-consciousness and is an actual experience as man — as ourselves.

69

When we think objectively, the object seems to be outside ourselves, or apart from us, and something that we think about. When we think objectively, it seems that we are growing up to some event, or advancing towards some condition, or that we are not being what we shall be later on. Objective thinking is very prevalent and should be replaced with subjective thinking. In true thinking, or subjective thinking, all objects or things are ideas, and we are these ideas. In subjective thinking we do not pass through material conditions or grow up to events, but we are the conditions or the events subjectively, and they are good and eternally good.

Church, a Subjective Experience

Every experience in our lives should be a subjective experience and especially should church be a subjective experience. Why? Because church, in its true meaning, is Christ, and Christ is comprised of the reality of every existing thing, and is man in God's image and likeness.

Mrs. Eddy defines church as "whatever rests upon and proceeds from divine Principle." Let us note the word whatever. Whatever means there is nothing in man or the universe, when rightly interpreted, that does not rest upon and proceed from divine Principle. Therefore church, or Christ, or man, "is the full representation of Mind," and is everything Mind is.

In the definition of church we should also note the word from. Church proceeds from Principle and is not something apart from Principle that must grow up to Principle. That would be an objective experience. But church is always a subjective experience inherent within our God-mind, and is good and eternally good.

When we understand that church is a growth out from Mind, this understanding helps church maintenance as nothing else can. The highest and most practical contribution we can make to any church, is that we, within ourselves, are the living, universal Christ, or church, or man. When we attain this exalted realization

70

of church, above the old objective sense of church, this realization precludes the human mind's pictures of lack along any line, and we find that all things exist and are present in faultless perfection and abundance.

The very nature of church, being the structure of Truth and Love, must be peace and plenty, must be prosperity and completeness, must be unfailing and unending, must be the spontaneous mental activity of all men. Our church is established within us subjectively — within our forever living Christ-consciousness. Church and all the activities of our church organization are mental — divinely mental — and these activities are always subjective experiences, inherent in true consciousness. If we fail to understand this, our church activities become restricted through the so-called laws of material planning, or through the so-called laws of objective thinking.

When working mentally for our church, if our thinking about church is objective — that is, if we are working up to some event — our demonstration will be obstructed and void. In order to have our work effective we must lift our thought above the material concept of church and church activities, and let it rest upon that which is primal and subjective. Then we find our church and all of its activities as good, and eternally good.

The real purpose of church is to elevate the human race by rousing it out of its dormancy, and to help the human mind yield to the divine, so that the divine is realized as the all and the only of our being. It is not the material church building with which we are primarily concerned. (See *Miscellany* 162:21.) The church of God is not a building. The more thoroughly we understand what church is, and what activities are, the less laborious church building becomes; then the process of church building proceeds with less effort and more joy; and better workmanship will be our material symbol.

It is the failure of Christian Scientists to perceive church in its true idea, as being the church of God, and as being a subjective experience, which accounts for the sense appearance of an imperfect church. We should cease working for church and church activities according to the usual, tiresome, human routine, and the usual sense of church as material and objective. We should refuse to accept the worn-out notion that a Christian Scientist is a personal worker, trying to fix things up. The divine Mind is the only worker, and an actual scientific treatment is God, divine Mind, in operation — Mind manifesting itself in full measure of realization and resistless power.

It is the smallness of our own concept of church which depicts everything materially, and limits our abundance of good. Our actual prosperity is in the realm of fundamental thinking, and our consciousness — the consciousness of divine Love — is capable of expressing itself in infinite measure. Our consciousness is the most dynamic activity in operation today, and everything is subject to our own right thought.

We hear the word need used excessively in almost every conversation. We talk about our need, the church's need, the civic need, the nation's need, the world's need. But, as Christian Scientists, we should understand that any thought of need is always error, and that error's need is nothing. Need, when seen subjectively and correctly interpreted, is always supply.

The welfare of our Cause is in the hands of Christian Scientists, and our Cause is a universal Cause. The welfare of the world and the welfare of our individual universe is in our hands. Our daily work for our church and our Cause should not be individual only, but it should be universal as well; it should be from the viewpoint that our church and our Cause are subjective, or are inherent in divine consciousness. Our thinking along all lines should be subjective thinking. If subjective thinking is uppermost in our thought, the reward will be great indeed.

2. AGGRESSIVE MENTAL SUGGESTION

The Belief that Evil Exists

No doubt everyone in this Association is convinced, through reason, revelation and logic, that there can be no such thing as evil or imperfection in the infinite consciousness. And we all see, intellectually at least, that it is utterly impossible for evil to have source, origin, or cause, and that it is utterly impossible for evil to come into existence in and of itself, or introduce itself into our consciousness.

Mrs. Eddy says, "The origin of evil is the problem of ages. It confronts each generation anew. It confronts Christian Science. The question is often asked, If God created only the good, whence comes the evil?

"To this question Christian Science replies: Evil never did exist as an entity. It is but a belief that there is an opposite intelligence to God. This belief is a species of idolatry, and is not more true or real than that an image graven on wood or stone is God.

"The mortal admission of the reality of evil perpetuates faith in evil; and the Scriptures declare that 'to whom ye yield yourselves servants to obey, his servants ye are.' This leading, self-evident proposition of Christian Science, that, good being real, its opposite is necessarily unreal, needs to be grasped in all its divine requirements." (*Miscellaneous Writings*)

It does seem at times that evil is very prevalent and very real, and it seems to have supremacy over good. Now, the cause of all this seeming is that we have been educated to believe that there is a power besides God, good — an evil power.

As soon as a child is born, the mother begins — and rightly so — to protect her child from danger, and thereby she teaches her child in a measure that evil is something to be avoided. The mother sees that her child does not fall, that it is not burned, does not eat anything that might harm it, and so on. Mrs. Eddy says, "The mother, guided by love, faithful to her instincts, and adhering to the imperative rules of Science, asks herself: Can I teach my child the correct numeration of numbers and never name a cipher? Knowing that she cannot do this in mathematics, she should know that it cannot be done in metaphysics, and so she should definitely name the error, uncover it, and teach truth scientifically." (*Miscellany*)

So since our babyhood we have been taught to believe that there are two opposing powers, one good and the other evil, and this false education has become entrenched — yes, almost incarnate — in our thinking, so that we see and hear evil on every side. We say that we do not believe in the power and presence of evil; and intellectually we do not; and, in fact, we are believing in the power of evil less and less. But if we really understood that God is All, we would not be here at this meeting today in order to gain more enlightenment on this subject. The allness of God is, and it is up to us to prove the powerlessness, yes, the unreality and nothingness of seeming evil. Since we have been educated into the belief of an evil power, we must now be educated out of the belief. We must unwind our snarls (our beliefs), and we do this by educating ourselves in the Science of good — through enlightenment and understanding, through spiritualization of thought, through consecration and persistent effort — until the victory is won on the side of Truth and good.

Mrs. Eddy tells us, "[Evil] needs only to be known for what it is not; then we are its master, not servant." "Evil is a negation: it never started with time, and it cannot keep pace with eternity." She says, "Not to know that a false claim [of evil] is false, is to be in danger of believing it; hence the utility of knowing evil aright, then reducing its claim to its proper denominator, — nobody and nothing." She makes these statements in *Miscellaneous Writings*.

To know evil aright we should know that evil is never an entity — that is, it is never a person or thing that is outside of us; it can never attack us from the external. We should know that all there is to evil is the outpicturing of a mental image of the so-called mortal mind.

74

We should know that no matter how vividly the image appears as persons or things or untoward conditions, it is always mortal mind seeing its own outpictured finite forms, its own thought-forms, or false conceptions. These outpictured thought-forms are illusions or delusions — they are images of matter held subjectively in mortal mind, but seen objectively by this mind.

We should know that all objectifications of evil are false mental pictures or images. They are illusions, and are never formed within God, Mind, consciousness — our Mind — any more than two plus two are five is formed within the science of mathematics. So-called mortal mind urges us to accept these mental illusions which appear externally to us as entities, when in fact they are simply adverse thoughts of a suppositional mind. So-called mortal mind is very suggestive in its urge that we accept its adverse thought as true thought.

There is but one way evil can reach us, and that is through the mental, just as two plus two are five reaches us through the mental. Whether the thought is sickness, sin, loss, poverty, war, disaster, calamity, accident, age or death, if such adverse thoughts reach us at all, they reach us through the mental. It is the mental suggestion that induces us to accept these thoughts as entities, and as something apart from and external to us.

We are all familiar with the verse in Deuteronomy that reads: "The Lord [that is, Truth or divine Mind] shall cause thine enemies that rise up against thee to be smitten before thy face: they shall come out against thee one way, and flee before thee seven ways."

This verse means that there is but one way by which evil or error can reach us, and this one way is through mental suggestion. All evil or error operates the same way, no matter what its form may be. Its approach is never in any form other than this one way — aggressive mental suggestion.

I want to emphasize the fact that evil or error of any nature operates invariably as suggestion. It matters not if it is family trouble,

75

or church trouble, or business trouble — these are suggestions, all mental pictures, formed within the human mind. They are never entities nor realities. All there is to suggestion is a false thought about some spiritual reality. Our false mental picture acts as an adverse influence on our so-called human consciousness, and causes the balance of influence to be on the side of evil suggestion, rather than on the side of reality. Our human thought is beginning to recognize this, and we are more and more defending ourselves against aggressive mental suggestions.

Someone may ask, Why do evil suggestions come to us? They come to us because we believe in evil. As long as we believe in evil, evil suggestions will come to us. Mrs. Eddy says, "Error comes to us for life, and we give it all the life it has" (from a letter quoted in *The Christian Science Journal*, August 1912, in an article "No Evil Power.")

It is our belief in evil as entity that causes us to respond to the suggestions of fear, jealousy, sickness, pain, poverty, age, war, and so on. It is our individual belief in the reality of these things that causes us to respond to these suggestions, and they immediately determine our so-called suffering; whereas we, as Christian Scientists, should rise above these suggestions and not be influenced by them. If we respond to them, then our thoughts become confused, we do not think clearly, and we are not able to do our work at hand in the best way. We need to be awake to the malpractice within our own thinking. This is all the malpractice there is — the malpractice within our own mentality.

Handling Aggressive Mental Suggestion

It is not so much our lack of understanding that makes aggressive mental suggestion hard to handle, but it is the unwillingness of the human mind to yield its belief in evil. The more aggressive these suggestions are, the more mesmeric they seem to be. They at times seem to take possession of our thinking. We all know how unwilling mortal mind is to yield its belief of lack, fear, war, pain, sickness, old age, or death. Mortal mind says "These things are so, because I see, feel and experience these things, and therefore they must be real." And yet all these things mortal mind sees, feels and experiences as real are just mental suggestions, and are as substanceless as the mirage of water on the highway ahead of the motor car.

We all know how persistent mortal mind is in its belief that there is no activity in business. Mortal mind says, and says it emphatically: Why, there is no business, and then proceeds to mesmerize itself with self-made mental conditions. It says, Under these circumstances, it is impossible for business to operate. Yes, mortal mind makes and sees and feels and experiences its own 'no business,' and when we try to turn away from these falsities, we see how unwilling mortal mind is to accept the truth that business, being divinely mental, is therefore always active and always good.

We all know how mortal mind persists in its belief that there is inability, incapacity, insufficiency and incompleteness. But the most unyielding mesmerism of mortal mind is its belief that there is a selfhood apart from God; its belief that individual man is a person, a corporeal material mortal with life and intelligence within himself; its belief that mortals can rob each other, and hinder each other, and displace each other, and think evilly of each other, and disturb and control each other's mentalities, thereby producing inharmonious conditions on the body. Mortal mind's self-love seems adamant. Is it any wonder Jesus said, "If any man will come after me, let him deny himself"?

These aggressive mental suggestions, if accepted as real, always leave a marked effect upon us individually; they not only dull our thinking, but they cause us to become negative, sleepy and indifferent to things in general. When we hold to the mortal mind suggestions that we have a material, personal existence, and a personal, restricted mind with which to apprehend all that is, we at once lose our standard of divine Science, and cease to apprehend all from the standpoint of divine Mind and through divine Mind.

Mrs. Eddy says in *Science and Health*, "If mortal mind knew how to be better, it would be better." One of the chief functions of Christian Science is to inform mortal mind, or this false personal mind, how to be better. We, who are enlightened with divine Science, know how to be better; and instead of being a stiff-necked and rebellious people clinging tenaciously to the testimony of the senses, we should turn from these suggestions and demonstrate the spiritual facts of existence.

The way to do this is, first, to realize the omnipotence, omnipresence, and omniscience of perfection. Then from this standpoint of the all of perfection, we let our affirmations and denials reduce that which claims to be a person with a belief of sin or sickness, to a belief without an identity. Then we inform this belief that it is only a finite, imperfect concept of a reality at hand; we are willing to give up the belief, and immediately we apprehend the perfect reality at hand.

Students, we are free to experience the allness of good, and when we once fully understand the illusory nature of aggressive mental suggestions — that they have no power, no substance, and no place — then these suggestions will have no power over us, or anybody, or anything. They are utterly false and ungrounded. They cannot touch us unless we accept them into consciousness as real, and identify them as person, power, or presence.

Let us clearly understand that suggestion is not thought; it is not idea; it is not intelligence. Aggressive mental suggestions are not formed by God, Mind, and are not subjectively in God, Mind; but our thoughts are formed by God, Mind, and therefore they cannot be touched by any evil suggestions. Suggestion or adverse thought — being no thought, having no source — cannot disturb our thinking, and thereby produce discordant phenomena on our bodies.

The suggestions that seem to assail us so aggressively are often undestroyed qualities in our thinking, either known or unknown — some longing, some fear, or some belief — which, when Truth and Love unfold in our consciousness, are brought to the surface, so that we may be delivered from them.

Jesus' temptations, as recorded in the fourth chapter of Luke, cover all the aggressive mental suggestions that can ever assail us. We read, "And Jesus being full of the Holy Ghost . . . was led by the Spirit [not by the devil, but by the Spirit] into the wilderness." The wilderness according to the "Glossary" in *Science and Health* is "the vestibule in which a material sense of things disappears, and spiritual sense unfolds the great facts of existence."

The Holy Ghost, or the unfoldment of Truth and Love, that came to Jesus at the time of his baptism, uncovered the material sense of things which was still latent in his consciousness, and it is this material sense which the devil or aggressive mental suggestion claimed to use when tempting Jesus during his forty days in the wilderness.

This material sense of things was uncovered to Jesus because of his higher understanding of Truth and Love, but as yet he had not demonstrated his ascension over them. The temptation or aggressive mental suggestion could not have touched Jesus, had he risen above the material sense of things, but the temptation came because this material sense of things was still in his consciousness undestroyed.

And if temptations or aggressive suggestions seem to mesmerize us, we may rest assured that it is the Holy Ghost or unfoldment of Truth and Love that is uncovering and bringing to the surface some deep-seated, erroneous and material sense of things in our consciousness that is yet undestroyed. We should not murmur, or grieve, or feel self-pity, or be discouraged, when these deeper errors are uncovered for us to destroy. Rather should we rejoice that Truth and Love are unfolding in our individual consciousness, and co-existently in the universal consciousness.

Maintaining the Spiritual Fact

Let us, like Jesus, stand the test and not be mesmerized by the suggestions that claim to be in the universal consciousness. It is true that as we demonstrate our ascension over these claims of aggressive mental suggestion in our individual consciousness, we are at the same time helping to overcome these similar aggressive suggestions in the universal consciousness.

Just as divine ideas exist in the infinite Mind and as Mind, subjectively, before they unfold objectively as concrete things, so, as Truth and Love unfold in our thinking, the material sense of things, latent in our consciousness, becomes aggressively apparent. But these unfoldments of Truth and Love are delivering us from the mesmeric beliefs; and if we are faithful to the higher facts of existence, as was Jesus, we shall little by little demonstrate our ascension over these beliefs and work out our own salvation.

Let us as Christian Scientists maintain our balance on the side of the Christ-consciousness, so that we may stand in the time of temptation. Jesus' consciousness was filled with the Holy Ghost, and as we maintain this altitude of thought, we find that with every aggressive suggestion we master, there is less suggestion and a greater unfoldment of Truth and Love. And like Jesus, when the devil has ended all the temptations, we shall be "in the power of the Spirit."

It is not only an interesting fact, but a very significant one, that the ability to detect and defend themselves from mental suggestions and mesmerism is required of all the men who are in the service of the British Navy. These men are taught to thwart the effects of mesmeric suggestions. They are taught to turn their thought from the suggestion, and place it upon an established fact — something they know to be true, even if it is only the multiplication table. They are taught never to yield to mesmeric suggestion, and never to go to sleep until the mesmerism is broken.

Since this indicates how important it is to take this stand in human affairs, it is imperative that a Christian Scientist should recognize the great necessity of mentally maintaining the spiritual fact in the face of aggressive suggestion of sense testimony.

We can readily see that the method used by the British Navy, though patterning the divine, is not sufficient. These men work from a material standpoint only; they do not have the divine unfoldment of spiritual reality wherewith to prove the unreality and nothingness of mesmeric suggestion. But if we, as Christian Scientists, made it a point never to go to sleep until we had broken the mesmerism or mesmeric suggestions that so aggressively assail us, we would be worth as much to the Cause of Christian Science as the British Navy is to their country. To do this means consecration to the Christ-consciousness that is within us.

In her *Message to The Mother Church for 1901*, Mrs. Eddy says, "Take possession of sin [which is aggressive mental suggestion] with such a sense of its nullity as destroys it." She also says in the textbook, "The relinquishment of error deprives material sense of its false claims." To be obedient to these requirements of divine Science, we find that it means a most rigid mental discipline, especially in these days when the so-called mortal mind is so greatly mesmerized. But let us remember that no matter how mesmeric the suggestion seems to be, our unfoldment of Truth and Love will reveal the divine reality — about which the suggestion is merely a suggestion — until finally the mesmerism melts away in the presence of the spiritual sense of things.

All there is to suggestion is our false mental sense about something that is divinely beautiful in its reality. Mental suggestion is but our educated belief that there is an opposite intelligence to God. This false mental sense which we entertain acts as an adverse influence on our so-called human consciousness, and causes the balance of influence to be on the side of the false mental picture, rather than on the side of reality. In order to defend ourselves against aggressive mental suggestion, our defense must be a

81

mental defense, or a mental protest, and it must operate within our own mentality.

All aggressive mental suggestions are the result of an educated belief that there are minds many, and the belief that all thinking is done in and of a personal mind. There is nothing that so restricts the realization of our true spiritual state as to be mesmerized with the aggressive mental suggestion that we are personal thinkers and that everyone else is also a personal thinker.

Most of the time we are mesmerized to the hilt with what we believe other persons are thinking. We are not only concerned about what others are thinking, but we are greatly concerned how their thinking may affect us, or affect our happiness, or influence our activities — especially if we think their thinking is adverse to our thinking. How little of the time we realize the inviolate fact that there is but one thinking agent — the divine Mind; and how little we realize that our own individual thinking is the showing forth of the thinking that the divine Mind is doing or being.

What appears to be personal thinking and doing is not personal thinking or doing even in belief. Personal thinking and doing is never person, but is the aggressive mental suggestion of a suppositional mortal mind. What appears to be personal thinking and doing, is simply the divine Mind's thinking and doing misrepresented. And no matter whether these aggressive mental suggestions seem to be our own thinking and doing, or another's thinking and doing, they are wholly mortal mind's suggestions. But if we accept these adverse thoughts and are influenced or mesmerized by them, then we are the victims of aggressive mental suggestions.

Each one of us is responsible for his own condition of thought. When we see what is called another's thinking and doing, it is our own so-called mind seeing its own thinking and doing. Each one of us sees only the quality and content of his own so-called mind. At times it may seem that we are so mesmerized with some adverse thought or distressing mental suggestion, and so mesmerized with our fear and worry of it, that we actually feel the distress that we are thinking, and thereby some physical trouble seems to be objectified or outpictured on our body.

Handling So-called Physical Problems

All there is to so-called physical disorders is fear or worry or adverse thinking seen and felt objectively. There is no such thing as physical or bodily disease. The seeming physical or bodily disease is never physical or bodily. It is purely so many mesmerized states. And because disease is not physical, but is mental in its nature and origin, its diagnosis must be mental and its method of healing must be mental.

All there is to our so-called physical ills, is our seeming ability to become so mesmerized with adverse thought that we feel this disturbed thought, and thereby our feelings are objectified or outpictured as so-called physical ills. It is self-evident that the actual claim for which we should be treated is our own mesmerism of some aggressive mental suggestion. It may be that we have accepted some individual's thinking as our own thinking.

Suppose all the world thinks or believes that I can have heart trouble. I cannot have heart trouble unless I think I can, or accept the mental suggestion that it is possible for me to have heart trouble. And suppose I really seem to have heart trouble, because the adverse thought that I have accepted as my thought is objectified or outpictured as heart trouble.

Heart trouble is not the actual claim, but mesmerism or hypnotism is the actual claim for which I need to be treated. It is the mesmeric thought of the whole world claiming to mesmerize me into thinking what others think. And this false claim never could be objectified as my heart trouble, if I did not accept the claim as my own thinking and fear it. Even if the whole world thinks that I have heart trouble, this malpractice or aggressive mental suggestion of mortal mind is powerless to make me think erroneously, and in this way, cause so-called physical ills on my body. Let us not forget we are free thinking agents — free to think as Mind.

It is not sufficient to treat or deny that I have heart trouble, because I have no heart trouble. My heart was in the beginning held subjectively within its cause, and there it remains today. What seems to be my heart trouble, is my mesmerized state or disturbed thought seeing and feeling itself. My seeming heart trouble is purely mesmeric suggestion — that is all there is to my heart trouble. The claim that I am mesmerized with the world's thinking that I can have heart trouble, or can be mesmerized by my belief that I do have it, is what must be handled specifically. My seeming heart trouble is in no way connected with my heart, but is purely an experience of mortal mind.

It is not enough just to declare that my seeming claim of heart trouble is unreal, or that it is only a lie, or that there is no truth in it, no reality in it; that is not enough to meet the claim unless my understanding of reality is great enough to wipe out, all at once, the whole claim of mesmeric suggestion. I must see that mesmerism is doing all of this — that aggressive mental suggestion is manufacturing my so-called heart trouble, and all its material accompaniments. If I have accepted all these adverse thoughts, and have become influenced by them, then I am the victim, not of my body which is purely spiritual, but of mental suggestion of supposititious mortal mind.

Just denying the claim is not enough, and this is far too common a tendency among Christian Scientists. My seeming heart trouble is a mesmeric mental condition, and I must deny that such a mesmeric state is possible. The aggressive mental suggestion of inaction, over-action, cessation of action, or impaired action, must be treated specifically as mental suggestion, and not as the objectified symptoms called heart trouble. The aggressive mental suggestions that are mesmerizing me must be discerned and uncovered in my own thinking, and are to be melted away by the unfoldment of Truth and Love in my own thinking.

The Christ-consciousness

We are our own saviour. "Where the Spirit of the Lord is, (that is, where these unfoldments of Truth and Love are) there is liberty." We must refuse to think that there is such a thing as mental malpractice, or adverse thought, or that we can be mesmerized by malicious mental suggestions. Truth and Love, being infinite, are all that is going on. And since Truth and Love bring to the surface these aggressive mental suggestions, then Truth and Love master them.

We know that the belief in aggressive mental suggestions is false, even if we seem to be mesmerized at times with these suggestions. Divine Science has revealed their falsity to us. Therefore the important thing for us to do is to discern and understand and declare that we, as the Christ-consciousness — or anyone else as the Christ-consciousness — cannot be made to believe in material suggestions such as jealousy, criticism, fear, worry and doubt, and objectify them.

When we clearly discern the falsity of the claims of aggressive mental suggestion or adverse thought, this discernment will prevent the seeming influence of error's ways of thinking. To discern and uncover and prove the nothingness of these claims is the work of every Christian Scientist. We should not only do this for ourselves and for our patients, but we should help our patients to do this for themselves. We heal our patients by handling the claim of aggressive mental suggestion — that is, by making nothing of these claims entirely within our own consciousness. The more we make nothing of these claims for ourselves, the more we make nothing of these claims for everyone else in the radius of our thinking.

Aggressive mental suggestion or adverse thought is "the prince of this world" and has nothing in us. There is nothing in our Christ-consciousness to respond to it. These seeming mental suggestions cannot do a thing to our Christ-consciousness. As we know that we are the Christ-consciousness, this knowing is the Christ-consciousness that breaks down every mesmeric suggestion of fear, and reigns supreme in Love. Knowing that we are the Christ-consciousness frees us and vanquishes every seeming discord and inharmony. There is no other way under heaven whereby we can be saved except the Christian Science method, which is to maintain our Christ-consciousness as the only consciousness.

We understand that aggressive mental suggestions are not something to be combated, and it is our work as Christian Scientists to discern the nothingness of mental suggestions — to understand that mesmerism is not power, because there is only one power. Aggressive mental suggestions have no cause, substance, or law; therefore they have no power to act or to be; and we of the Christ-consciousness should not give them power or presence. Aggressive mental suggestions are void of intelligence, because they are only adverse thoughts of a supposititious mind. They are not Mind, therefore they cannot act as Mind or cause, neither can they be objectified as effect. They have no substance wherein to act upon the Christ-consciousness. They have no law or Principle to support them or to enforce themselves.

Mrs. Eddy in the following citations has eliminated entirely every reason for giving these seeming suggestions power or entity. In *Miscellaneous Writings*, she says, "'The Lord reigneth; let the earth rejoice.' No evidence before the material senses can close my eyes to the scientific proof that God, good, is supreme. Though clouds are round about Him, the divine justice and judgment are enthroned."

Again in *Miscellany* she says, "Lest human reason becloud spiritual understanding, say not in thy heart: Sickness is possible because one's thought and conduct do not afford a sufficient defense against it . . . Only he who learns through meekness and love the falsity of supposititious life and intelligence in matter, can triumph over their ultimatum, sin, suffering, and death."

3. CHRISTIAN SCIENCE PRACTICE

Question and Answer on Hearing

We will consider today a question sent to me by a student. Since the answer includes several vital points in the practice of Christian Science, I asked this student if I might discuss it before the Association.

"Dear Mrs. Wilcox: I should like to have some helpful thoughts in regard to hearing. I have seemed to have a condition of impaired hearing to disturb my thought much too long. I have tried to realize perfection, but there seems to be something that stands in the way of my realization. I have heard others say, 'There is something in your own thought needs correcting.' But, Mrs. Wilcox, I could not agree with that statement. We know that God is All, and all means everywhere, and everywhere would certainly be in thought, and right where God is nothing else can be. Then I came across this beautiful thought that substantiated my conviction. The thought was this: 'There is no condition to be corrected; all one needs is enlightenment.' It also said, 'One does not take the position that the physical condition is the result of mental inharmony.' Since it is enlightenment I need, will you please give it to me?"

In answering this question, let us clearly understand that the claims of mortal mind are always beliefs, and we as Christian Scientists do not ignore a belief; but we do make a clear distinction between ignoring a belief and accepting a belief. In Christian Science practice we never ignore a belief of any kind, neither do we accept it. If we accept a belief as an entity, then we become the victim of the belief. This student has accepted the belief of impaired hearing, because she says, "I have seemed to have a condition of impaired hearing to disturb my thought too long." In Christian Science practice, we never ignore a belief. This student has not ignored the belief, but she has accepted it, and by accepting it in her thought as an entity, she became the victim of the belief.

87

She says, "We know that God is All, and all is everywhere, and everywhere must be in thought, and right where God is nothing else can be." This is excellent reasoning, but if this student fully realized her statement that God is everywhere — even the substance of her thought — she would have ascended above the mortal sense of this belief. This student should awaken to the fact that so long as she accepts the belief that she is in a state of impaired hearing, and must in some way get out of this state, she will remain the victim of her belief, because the experience of impaired hearing is simply the objectification of her adverse thinking about this claim.

The student should realize and maintain the fact that her Christ-consciousness is the presence of God, or fullness of joy. There is nothing in her Christ-consciousness that can sense impaired hearing. There was nothing in the Christ-consciousness of the Hebrew boys that could sense destructive flames. They had not accepted the adverse thought of destructive flames as their consciousness; therefore they were not the victims of that belief.

This student does not have to get out of this condition of impaired hearing. She is already out, because the Christ-consciousness is not in an inharmonious state of any kind. Reasoning in this manner, this student will cease accepting the claim of impaired hearing, because she is understanding herself as one with God, good.

This student should not ignore the claim, but she should handle it specifically according to the rules in the textbook. It may take much spiritualization of thought and a steadfast endeavor on her part to maintain the actual facts of her being, but Mrs. Eddy says, "Be active, [that is, be active in true thought] and, however slow, thy success is sure." (*Miscellaneous Writings*)

We, as students of Christian Science, know that the ear has nothing to do with this claim of impaired hearing. We are told in our textbook to "detach sense from the body, or matter, which is only a form of human belief, and you may learn the meaning of God, or good, and the nature of the immutable and immortal."

This student has accepted the educated thought of the whole world that her ear is material, and that she hears by means of a material ear; that her ear has become imperfect, and thereby her hearing has become impaired. She has accepted this thought as her thought, and it has worried her and disturbed her until she feels her own adverse thought objectified as impaired hearing. Now, a material ear does not hear. It is Mind only that hears. Not that Mind is a means of hearing, but Mind is an all-hearing Mind; and Mind to itself would have to become impaired before hearing could become impaired.

Ear is never material; this so-called material ear is only the human mind's wrong way of sensing a divine idea, and has nothing to do with the function of hearing. We do not have this idea to hear with, but we have ear as divine idea, because we spiritually understand true being. This divine idea — ear — forever expresses or shows forth the true hearing that divine Mind is being. This student has accepted the world's belief as her belief, and her thought has become mesmerized, and now she must demesmerize her thought. In order to do this, she must recognize that her individual consciousness is the Christ-consciousness and has never been touched by aggressive mental suggestion or adverse thoughts of so-called mortal mind. Her Christ-consciousness stands eternally as the Christ-consciousness, and nothing can be added to it or taken from it. It is inviolate.

In this process of de-mesmerizing consciousness, this student should handle specifically all the *materia medica* beliefs, which are the world beliefs or opinions of mankind about ear. She should understand and be thoroughly convinced that her ear is not a material thing, but a divine idea, wholly mental and wholly spiritual. If there seems to be a roaring in the head, etc., this student should handle the *materia medica* suggestion that the tympanum, or drumlike membrane in the ear, instead of remaining taut, has become sagged and does not allow enough air in the ear. This seeming condition is not supposed to impair the hearing even in belief.

Materia medica says this seeming condition is caused by intense mental strain. All these beliefs are so many kinds of mental mesmerism and should be handled, not as entities, but as belief only.

In Christian Science, we learn that this particular idea — ear — in order to be what it is in its character, and to have substance and existence, must have as its essence all the qualities of its cause or Mind. For being a divine idea, it has the intelligence of Mind, the substance of Spirit, the body of Soul, the creative power of Principle, the conscious omni-action of Life, the unalterableness of Truth, the knowing and feeling of Love. These characteristics of Deity are the essential qualities that give to this infinite idea — ear — its divine character, its substance and essence.

How enlarged is this idea, when "seen through the lens of Spirit"! Surely we cannot be mesmerized with the aggressive suggestion that ear is material and finite, or diseased, or inflamed, or swollen, or congested, or paralyzed, or imperfect. All these seeming sensations are not conditions of the ear, but are merely mesmerism and must be dealt with entirely in the mental.

This student took exception to the statement, "There is something in your own thinking that needs healing," on the ground that this statement did not tally with absolute Truth. I would like to say right here, let us be most careful never to recognize a mesmerism as personal. A mesmerism of any kind is never in nor of person, but is always mortal mind feeling its own subjective state, and seeing and feeling it objectified. If we see a claim as real and personal, either in ourselves or another, we are accepting the world's belief as our belief, and we make ourselves liable to that belief. We, as Christian Scientists, are to detect the errors of mortal mind as errors, therefore as nothing and nobody. God, good, is all.

Now this statement, "There is something in your own thought that needs correcting," was made from the standpoint of belief, and from this standpoint it was a true statement. From the belief standpoint this was the very thing that needed to be done. She needed to clear away the mesmerism in her own thought, because if the aggressive mental suggestion that mesmerized her to the extent that she felt impaired hearing, were discerned and uncovered as suggestion only, she would be de-mesmerized, and the healing would be instantaneous.

The aggressive mental suggestions that are mesmerizing the student must be discerned and uncovered in her own mentality, and must be melted away by the unfolding of Truth and Love in her thinking. Her belief in impaired hearing is a mesmeric mental condition, and it is through an understanding of divine Truth that she can deny that such a mesmeric state is possible.

This student also said, "One is not to take the position that the physical condition is the result of mental inharmony." Both the mental inharmony and the so-called physical condition are impossible from the standpoint of true being. But if this student takes the position, from the standpoint of belief, that she has a physical condition called impaired hearing, then she will take the position that her condition is the result of mental inharmony, because a so-called inharmonious physical condition is always a mental inharmony objectified. Since some adverse thought which this student has accepted, is disturbing her and is objectified as the physical inharmony of impaired hearing, then it is evident that this inharmony must be discerned and made extinct in her human consciousness by understanding the spiritual facts concerning God and man.

Speaking from the standpoint of fact, Mrs. Eddy says in the textbook, "Immortal Mind is the only cause; therefore disease is neither a cause nor an effect." Then speaking from the standpoint of belief she says, "False beliefs are the procuring cause of all sin and disease." In Christian Science practice, we know that claims of sickness do not exist; we know that all claims are wholly false mental pictures, false beliefs, mesmerism, and that they can be extinguished only in our own mentality. In this way, they will disappear from our bodies.

Then this student found this beautiful statement, "There is no condition to be healed; all that one needs is enlightenment."

91

Yes, in Truth, there is no condition to be healed, and all that this student needs is enlightenment. As her love for Truth becomes supreme in her affections, it will displace whatever is unlike Christ, first mentally, then physically. The recipe for all healing is spiritualization of thought, and there must be deep consecration and faithful study on our part in order to earn our understanding of Truth and demonstrate our true being.

The Necessity for Christian Science Healing

When we heal the sick, we are establishing the Cause of Christian Science. It is through our healing work that Christian Science is reaching all mankind, and will finally cover the whole earth. Healing the sick gives Christian Science permanence and strength, and to give Christian Science permanence and strength is the great purpose in our healing work.

It is absolutely essential, in this day and hour, for healing to be accomplished through Christian Science. The demand upon Christian Science is such that, in order to fulfill its purpose and accomplish its mission, we must rise to the realization that there is one Mind, and let that one Mind be the only Mind. This is self-denial, and Jesus said, "If any man will come after me, let him deny himself, and take up his cross, and follow me."

In our treatment we must see not only what Mind is, but we must see by means of Mind itself, and we must understand as Mind. We are apt to think *about* Mind, but we must think *as* Mind. If we think about Mind, that is simply suggestion; but if we think as Mind, then our thinking is spiritual law in operation. As our practice in Christian Science goes on, it is more and more possible, by means of the revelation of Christian Science, to exercise this divine power and think *as* Mind. It is not because we take a little divine power and do something with it in our treatment; but it is because our thought is like divine power that it has divine power.

We should give our treatment with the understanding that it

is God, or Mind, giving it, and that He knows how to give it. We should expect no other result than the presence of God and the evidence of God, but we should not look for results so much as we should know the results. When the false sense begins to lessen, we should not stop the treatment, but we should destroy the error of belief completely by knowing its nothingness, and we should keep on until there is not a vestige of the error left in evidence.

Do not be deceived. Do not take the attitude that the work is done while the evidence of the disease is still present. Stick to the case until the evidence of the disease has vanished completely. So long as the evidence is contrary to our treatment, our work is not finished. Sometimes we hear practitioners say, "I had the realization of God so well that the work is done." But if the patient is not well, he might say, "That is all very well for you, but what about me!"

A treatment in Christian Science affirms "perfect God and perfect man," and that is the foundation of our denial. A denial is virtually an affirmation. As we affirm or know, that which we affirm or know acts as a denial of that which is untrue or false. Our denial should never be a fight with a false claim. Our denial, if adequate, reduces the false claim to nothingness, and this is the only adequate denial that is made in Christian Science. We are all guilty of making such remarks as, I'll treat it (meaning the false claim) again tomorrow. Or, I'll go at it again in a short time. When we speak of a false claim in this manner, the claim is a reality — a real thing to us. But in an adequate denial there is nothing here, there, or anywhere, but the one Mind.

It is not enough to say, "There is no disease," or "Evil is not power," or "My body is not material," and still have the disease, the evil, or a material body present as a real thing in consciousness. It is not an adequate denial until we have the realization of the utter nothingness of disease, of evil, or of materiality — the realization of nothing apart from God. A claim is never a fact. A claim is not here or anywhere. It is not even something to be denied. It is not man. Our denial must reach this height in realization, or it is not a complete denial.

Our great temptation is to work through the divine Mind to cure some material thing, when there is no material thing. God is All. Our denial must be thorough, as if Mind made the statements; and if Mind made the statements, there would be nothing present but Mind. The result of all affirmations and denials should be "perfect God and perfect man."

In our practice work, we are not looking for results. We know what is. We give our treatment with no doubt about it. It is not so much that we are treating a patient, as it is that we are knowing the truth that is present. Our treatment is never given to make a patient well, but it is given to establish the fact that he *is* well. Through our treatment, we find that 'wellness' is all there is to his being. We always use the present tense in giving a treatment — man is always perfect now.

Essentials in Christian Science Treatment

There are three essentials in every treatment. We may not always say them in words, but they are present in a good treatment. These three essentials are: *cause, substance, law*. We establish these three essentials in every Christian Science treatment. Then the opposite claims of error must be denied specifically: the denial of the belief in a cause other than God; the denial of the belief in any substance other than Spirit; and the denial of the belief in any law but the law of Spirit. In every good treatment, there will also be these three denials.

In a Christian Science treatment, after we have established cause, substance and law, the first thing we handle is *fear*, because when we have established cause, substance and law, the thing that stands out is, "I am afraid," and while it is only a belief, yet the whole world thinks it. Having established the divine Mind as cause, substance and law, we understand that there is no fear in man.

Fear has no origin, no cause, no presence, no law. The claim of fear is a false claim without activity, being, law, or substance; without presence or place or occupancy. Being a false claim, it cannot prevent the instantaneous effect of a Christian Science treatment. We should always handle the fear of the patient, and also the fear of the person who is not the patient. In most cases, it is the mother or father or grandmother. So, in handling any case, we take cognizance of all that might interfere, and in this way we prevent the interference.

Mrs. Eddy says that we should have confidence and dominion in our treatment, that we should give a treatment as if it were power being exercised. The only way we can possess this confidence and dominion and power is for us to realize that our understanding — no matter how little it is — is God, or Truth, with us; and this little understanding is bigger than the beliefs of the whole world, and has more power than any material law. Yes, we should have the greatest confidence in our treatment. Jesus told us, "The Lord said unto my Lord [that is, my understanding], sit thou on my right hand, till I make thine enemies thy footstool."

Whenever we give a treatment, we should always establish the law of God for the particular thing we are treating. To establish the law of God for any particular claim, means to establish the truth about that particular claim. Mrs. Eddy says in *Unity of Good*, "Truth is God, and in God's law. This law declares that Truth is All, and there is no error. This law of Truth destroys every phase of error."

Students of Christian Science know that active, unalterable, conscious Truth, as our own consciousness, is what constitutes God's law in us. Conscious Truth is all that is going on at any time or in any place; and conscious Truth is going on as law, as that which never varies or changes.

Let us take a case of cancer and apply the law of God to it. Since we know that conscious Life or Spirit is the one and only substance of all things, then God's law governing this particular case is that conscious Life or Spirit is the substance of each and every cell and tissue in this case. And since conscious Life is the only substance, and this substance is sustained by God's law, then there never was, is not now, nor ever can be, broken down cells.

Each and every cell and tissue is living conscious substance, conscious Life, conscious omni-action eternally. Each and every cell forever verifies the law of God in that all substance is incorruptible, indestructible, changeless and eternal. The one and only substance is always perfect as God is perfect. And we have the further statement of fact from the Psalmist David, that God will not suffer His Holy One — that is, His idea of Himself — to see corruption. (See Psalm 16:10.) What has never been seen or known of God, has never existed in manifestation or man.

Enlarging the Area of Practice

In our healing work, our thought should be enlarged so that we may bring every thought into subjection to the Christ. It is imperative that we, as Christian Scientists, should enlarge our vision and broaden the base of our thinking in order that we may be active workers in our Cause. By way of illustration, I want to say a few words about our attitude of thought towards the various means of transportation in the world today.

If we listen to the general conversation, we hear that mortal mind is arranging for accidents all the time and expecting them. We hear of them on every side. Even Christian Scientists are prone to tell about their accidents and make the incidents pretty big. They seem to think that it gives them a kind of distinction.

Now a train, a bus, an automobile or an airplane are perfectly natural and desirable things to have. There is nothing in religion or Science that would deprive us of these things. They should add greater and fuller abundance in our living, and give us greater peace and security.

These things are most desirable; and we, as Christian Scientists, should maintain our trains, automobiles, airplanes in absolute security; and there should be no unnatural wearing out or disintegration of these things. And there would be no unnatural wearing out and breakage of these things if we interpreted them as Love's or Mind's ideas, and not as the material things they seem to be. We learn from our Bible that the children of Israel wandered forty years in the wilderness, and their shoes waxed not old.

If we perceive, even in a small degree, the nature of divine Science and its divine character of indestructibility, then when we demonstrate an automobile or any other means of transportation, we should demonstrate its indestructibility also. These human concepts or material modes of transportation that appear to meet our needs in everyday living, have greatly changed in form and power during the past ten years, and no doubt will change more and more and appear better as they approach reality.

There is an urgent need for healing within ourselves of our false attitude towards these conveniences. We should cease thinking of them as the material things they appear to be. These human concepts, when correctly understood, are divine ideas; and when so interpreted, they will always bless us and contribute to our well-being.

Because we continue to put cause, substance and law in matter or material things, we still continue to view these means of transportation from a material standpoint. It is our false viewpoint that makes these things appear material with material accompaniments; and then we automatically place them under material laws — the so-called laws of accidents, destruction, disintegration, decay, impermanency and annihilation. And while the so-called laws of matter are belief only, yet if they are not dispelled by the apprehension that substance is Spirit, and by the understanding of spiritual law, these modes of transportation will continue to be governed wrongly to their ultimate discord and destruction.

The evil or material sense that we entertain in regard to transportation, does not require matter or material things through

97

which to express itself. No! Evil or material sense is itself all there is to matter or the material thing. The evil or material sense in connection with transportation requires belief only, and this belief fulfills all its own inharmonious conditions, all in consonance with its belief that matter is substance, that cause is in matter, that mind is mortal, and that law is the activity of mortal mind.

Transportation of any kind, when considered as material, is illusion. In other words, these conveniences express only the material sense of what is actually present as the divine idea of substance, permanency, completeness, wholeness, satisfaction, ease — ideas which contribute to a perfect state of being. Again I say, there is great necessity in changing our viewpoints from belief to understanding in order to experience the blessings that these things bring us.

Everything Governed by Divine Law

If all the inventions and conveniences that have been brought to light through the cultivation of human intelligence had appeared as the result of our recognition and demonstration of divine ideas, instead of the material things that they seem to be, perfection and completeness would be the law of every one of them. Recognized and demonstrated as divine ideas, we would soon find that the so-called laws of matter governing these inventions, would give place to divine law, and while an airplane would come down, it could not fall down, and while various vehicles could move upon the earth to the great convenience of mankind, they could not collide nor operate in any way contrary to perfection, because the reciprocal law of divine being is everywhere in operation.

If we find ourselves in the presence of a great congestion or sudden danger, it is our work to see at once what governs. There is not one car governed by mortal mind and another car governed by divine Mind. There is only one Mind and every car is governed by the law of this one Mind. The only driver there is, is divine Mind, and He drives every car, and He makes no mistakes.

Dr. Lyman Powell, author of *Mary Baker Eddy, A Life Size Portrait*, quotes her as saying, "Things are not what they seem. They are figures of the true. If our faith were but more simple, we would see them as they are, expressions of the divine, in forms we call material."

When we demonstrate Christian Science along any line, let us remember that we are demonstrating in behalf of humanity. We are demonstrating not only for ourselves, but for all mankind. Whenever we declare the spiritual nature of man, let us make the law of Christian Science so practical that it is immediately available to the man who thinks he is material, as well as to ourselves who still appear to be material. We should have the truth so clear, so absolute, and so established in our thought that it is instantly available, like two plus two equals four is instantly available.

We are Christian Scientists, and we do not just happen to do these things. Our trains, our houses, our businesses, our money, our cars — they are all held in the divine order of Science, governed by this Science, controlled by this Science, regulated by its law.

Jesus came to the world and proved the power of Spirit over the flesh, and demonstrated that divine law was available to man, that it healed the sick, saved the sinner, raised the dead and did everything that ought to be done, just as if God were present and had done it. And God *is* present and doing it, because there is no other God but a present God, and what appears to be going on as accidents or inharmonies is not happening. If they appear to have presence and power, they still are not happening. We, as Christian Scientists, should maintain this perfect poise of divine being so fixed in our consciousness, and as our consciousness, that nothing can mar or disturb it.

Mrs. Eddy says that we are to find all in God. And when we do our healing work in this way, we are beginning to function in Christian Science, and will have results commensurate with our understanding. We will find encouragement, happiness and peace in our work, and our practice will not be so difficult.

99

Being a Christian Science Practitioner

Since we are all practitioners in a greater or lesser degree, I want to talk a little about practitioners. We, as practitioners, should have newness of life. We should never let our declarations of Truth become stale. We should keep them fresh with new ideas continually flowing in; we should look upon our inspiration as unfolding inspiration bestowed directly upon us by divine Mind. Each patient we treat is entitled to fresh inspiration. In *No and Yes* Mrs. Eddy says, "Truth cannot be stereotyped; it unfoldeth forever."

This inspiration is a steady influx of divine ideas — a new vision of the glories of real being — and brings transcendent healing. As we recognize that spiritual inspiration is the healing process, this recognition will result in more instantaneous healings. We should pray for new light on old passages, and we should find this new light streaming in from everywhere. With new light and fresh inspiration, our treatments do not become dulled from much use and constant repetition. We should pray often for new light and continuous inspiration.

In the *Manual* we find that formulas are forbidden. This is because formulas stupefy our thought and hinder the unfoldment of inspiration from the divine Mind. We have our books; let us study them.

It is not only necessary that practitioners should have inspiration, but it is also necessary to have spiritual discernment. Jesus, with the Christ-consciousness, saw instantly what the human mind was thinking, and saw the nothingness of it. Mrs. Eddy says in the textbook, "You will reach the perfect Science of healing when you are able to read the human mind after this manner and discern the error you would destroy."

It is necessary to see what others are thinking; or rather, it is necessary to perceive the thinking that mortal mind is doing, the thinking that is trying to mesmerize both practitioner and patient.

We need not concern ourselves about the person who seems to be doing the thinking; it is always mortal mind operating as aggressive mental suggestion that is mesmerizing the patient. The practitioner needs to discern this false belief of mortal mind and prove its unreality and nothingness, thereby freeing the patient.

What we, as practitioners, see and do and think about what another person is seeing, doing, and thinking, must be worked out in our own selves. We must solve this problem in our own thinking, never in another's thinking. It is aggressive mental suggestion that causes us to see another doing and thinking thus and so, when the Christ-consciousness alone is thinking and doing all things. Our work as practitioners is to be this Christ-consciousness and to see the perfect man all the time.

The Christian Science practitioner must meet and overcome all seeming obstructions in his own experience and in the experience of others at the point of his own belief in them. At no other point do we have actual contact with the claim of evil. All temptations are at this point of our own consciousness, and here alone is where we overcome them.

We must make the demonstration that we are the Christ-consciousness, and that we stand as the Christ-consciousness — the only consciousness — under any seeming condition. This Christ-consciousness that we are, will break down every mesmeric suggestion of fear and will reign supreme as law. If we, in our own thinking, make the demonstration that we are the Christ-consciousness, this will solve every problem in another's personal thinking.

When we as practitioners discern what our patient or any other human being is thinking, we should be very sure that our discernment is always on a scientific basis. Mrs. Eddy tells us in the textbook, "It is recorded that Jesus, as he once journeyed with his students, 'knew their thoughts,' — read them scientifically. In like manner he discerned disease and healed the sick." Now, in order to read thoughts scientifically, we must never read them from the standpoint of minds many, but from the standpoint that divine Mind is the only thinking agent.

101

We can never proceed scientifically if we start from the standpoint that there is mortal mind thinking. To attempt to do so is no more Christian Science than would be the attempt to demonstrate mathematics from the standpoint of mistakes. Mrs. Eddy says Jesus read the minds of his students and he saw their sins, but he did not believe it was their minds, and this did the healing. Yes, Jesus saw their sins, but saw them simply as false beliefs or illusions; and he saw their minds as being the divine Mind, the only Mind.

How do we, as practitioners, get this discernment? How can we know what the erroneous thought is that is holding the patient? There is but one way to gain this discernment. We ask infinite Mind, infinite consciousness. We ask our own Mind — because Mind is the only consciousness there is — to reveal it to us. We could not ask mortal mind or aggressive mental suggestion to reveal this to us. We must ask Mind, the Christ-consciousness, just as we ask the principle of mathematics to reveal a mistake in our mathematical problem.

When we discern error through spiritual discernment, it never injures anyone, but blesses everyone. Surely it blesses one when the practitioner discerns the covering that needs to be removed from the face of the whole world, so that we see the face of our brother as the face of God. Such discernment would shorten the day of mesmerism that we seem to be experiencing.

All things that seem to be transpiring as our world, whether at home or abroad, whether the affairs are national or international, are never outside of us, where they are difficult to handle. They are here in our own consciousness as realities, and they need to be understood in their reality. In infinite consciousness "there is neither Jew nor Greek, there is neither bond nor free, there is neither male nor female: for ye are all one in Christ Jesus." Yes, all these in their true light are the sons and daughters of God, imperfectly known by us, because of mortal material sense. The textbook tells us, "Material sense defines all things materially."

Scientific Christianity demands that we affirm that what we see is divine, or is the son of God, here and now; and that we demonstrate this truth instead of merely believing in it, and demonstrate it to be a present fact here and now. This is our responsibility as individual Christian Scientists.

Mrs. Eddy refers to these days — meaning the days of mesmerism and hypnotism — that they should be shortened by Christian Scientists; and Jesus said, "Unless these days are shortened by the elect, no flesh would be saved." (See *Science and Health* 96:12-4; Matt 24:22). We, as working Christian Scientists, are the elect, and we should detect and uncover all adverse mesmeric thought — whether personal, national or world thought — and prove its unreality and nothingness. And we should do this detecting, uncovering and proving within our own thinking.

Slow Healing and Failures

I want to say something about cases of slow healing. If we, as practitioners, do not meet a claim in a reasonable time, or are not doing as well with the case as we would like, it might be well for us to ascertain something specific as to the nature of the claim, or learn what it is mortal mind says when it calls a disease blood pressure, or whooping cough, or cancer. I do not mean by this that you should have a medical diagnosis. The person who has any disease has it because of mortal mind, and never because of the human body; and mortal mind holds within itself all that the false claim is, including its name and all the beliefs connected with that name.

If we need to know specifically in regard to some form of error, we should do our work thoroughly from the standpoint of divine Principle and hold there, knowing that there is nothing wanting in our treatment, that our treatment is inspired of the divine Mind. In this way, all that is essential will come to light, sometimes in quite an astonishing way. All that we need to know will be uncovered through the action of Truth.

In every case we have, we should handle the different phases that seem to come up in connection with the case. In a case of rheumatism, we handle the belief that there are other beliefs following the original claim, such as pain and stiff joints. And we should also handle the belief that there was a cause, such as a run of fever, that could produce rheumatism in the first place.

If the patient comes to us the next day, after we have worked thoroughly for him, and says, "I am much worse," we should not treat rheumatism just at this time, but we should treat the belief that he is much worse, for this is the present claim. Or he might say, "This and this has occurred." Handle these phases of belief, and see that they do not extend or produce other beliefs. Of course, we continue our work on the original claim until it is met.

In giving a treatment, much depends on what the practitioner knows, and whether his understanding is entirely free from any belief of fear. A practitioner is not always to blame if he does not heal a case; but of this we may be sure, we should not make excuses for our failures.

It is much better not to say, "It was impossible to heal the case because he was so full of old theology." If he was full of old theology, and that was what was the matter with him, we should heal him of old theology. We sometimes hear practitioners say they could not do anything for a patient because he would not give up his drinking, or he was so stingy, or he had such an ugly disposition, or there was so much material resistance. If these were the claims, we should handle the claims and heal his beliefs. If our understanding is not sufficient to heal a case, it is much better not to make excuses or try to explain our failure. It is far better to say simply, "I'm sorry, but I didn't know enough."

It may seem to take time and much patience to work out some cases, but we are to keep on, as Isaiah says, "Until the cities be wasted without inhabitant [that is, until the false sense disappears, and until the mortal disappears from thought] and the houses without man" — which means until the material sense of a sick mortal disappears from thought.

If a practitioner who has been faithful should lose a case, he should not condemn himself; if he consecrated himself fully to work on the case, then he should not condemn himself. Mrs. Eddy admonishes us that we should not condemn ourselves, because the condemnatory thought closes the very door divine Love has provided for our escape. When we seem to have this cross to bear, we have this promise, "Surely he shall deliver thee from the snare of the fowler and from vain gossip." (Translated from the Arabic.)

To be really healed — that is, to be the Christ-consciousness — is something far greater and more blessed than any ease in matter. The need of this mental, spiritual, permanent healing is very great, and when we as Christian Scientists avail ourselves of this kind of healing, what is called physical healing will be simultaneously forthcoming.

"Love is the Fulfilling of the Law"

Paul, in the thirteenth chapter of Romans, urges upon the Church that its first duty is the consecration of Christian life and its service to mankind. This was a natural position for Paul to take in regard to one's duty, because all down the ages the thought of service has been inherent in our being. "Thou shalt love thy neighbor as thyself. Love worketh no ill to his neighbor: therefore love is the fulfilling of the law."

We all know that love is a wholly mental, spiritual activity of Mind. Love is divine Mind, our Mind, that thinketh no evil. Love is that quality of our own Mind that is constant, unchanging, ever yearning to help and to protect others. The Bible teaches that in order to fulfill the law of Love, we must bear one another's burdens. This Love is not a personal mind, neither is it for a few persons, but for all men. Love is the healing Christ and "is impartial and universal in its adaptation and bestowals."

The world is beginning to see that all its troubles are mental troubles; that its diseases are not physical, but mental in nature.

105

The world is seeing that its troubles are not so many physical ills, but so many mental mesmerisms; that we are no longer dealing with matter, but with mesmeric states of thought. As the individual and the world in general recognizes that all the inharmonies of the mind and body are mental in their nature and origin, they also realize that these inharmonies must be diagnosed mentally, and that the method of their healing must be Mind-healing.

Since all the world's troubles are mental and must be healed through Mind, and Mind in its nature is Love, then all healing is accomplished by loving, not condemning. According to the teachings of the Bible, we never permit our condemnation to rest upon anyone. Another's illusions or mesmerisms may seem to be many and very great in belief, but we who see as Mind, as Love, see their unreality and nothingness.

Since the only way we can serve mankind or bear one another's burdens is to do it mentally, and since we know that suggestions or adverse thoughts tend to deplete the one who takes them in, then when we see our neighbor taking in the suggestions of sickness and lack, aren't we fulfilling the law of Love when we know the unreality and nothingness of these things? It is by knowing the unreality and nothingness of any adverse thought which may be presented to our consciousness that we free both ourselves and our neighbor. By destroying these suggestions in mortal thought at the point of our own consciousness, we are helping to free all mankind.

In church matters, in home relations and business affairs, if we hold to the fact of Christian Science as stated in our textbook, "that all inharmony of mortal mind or body is illusion, possessing neither reality nor identity," this fact realized by us will fulfill the law of Love to our neighbor, and bear his burdens. But if we fail to put this fact into operation as our thought, then we are opening our consciousness to the suggestions of mortal mind that are sent out to deplete us and our neighbor. Let us be alert to recognize what mortal mind is thinking, and not let its suggestions interfere with our dominion or our neighbor's. It is our duty, as set forth by Paul, to be consecrated in our service to mankind.

Students, it is astonishing, when we begin to experience in Christian Science the power of Love, how we readily see that Mrs. Eddy does not exaggerate when she says that Love is that Mind that 'thinketh no evil', that is not dual; the Mind that is an active, conscious mode of Truth.

If Love is understood and demonstrated, we do not doubt about the outcome of anything; we need not fear that malpractice will interfere with our practice. Our practice will be all right as we demonstrate the Love that is God. Every difficulty that we encounter, since all is mental, will fade away in that presence which is Love; but that presence must be our Christ-consciousness.

Divine Love is the one power in the universe. It will do everything — heal the sick, save the sinner, cast out devils, help those who despair, comfort those who mourn, raise the dead, prevent dying and establish immortality. It behooves us, as Christian Scientists, to love more all the time, and then more and more.

We should not have any sentimentality about Love. Just love; be that creature that is ever kind, not only to man and woman, but to all creatures. Be that Love wherein no one is condemned, wherein no one is even for a single moment shut out of the kingdom of heaven, but always established and maintained in heaven, harmony.

There is nothing in the whole universe in the way of evil that can withstand our understanding and demonstration of divine Love. There is no evil too great or too strongly entrenched to withstand our demonstration of divine Love, and no one can possibly escape the redeeming influence of that thought which is "Love . . . reflected in love." The concrete evidences of divine Love, expressed humanly, are pure affection, protection, provision, consideration, thoughtfulness, kindness, and above all, graciousness. Like our Master, out of the amplitude of these qualities, let us define the words — divine Love.

ABOUT THE AUTHOR: The papers of Martha Wilcox deal with the subjective consciousness and how it can be changed through an understanding of God. Mrs. Wilcox shows that change is inevitable when we treat the inner self through prayer as taught in Christian Science. The strong point of her writing is her emphasis on the need to so spiritualize the subjective self that it results in healing.

Martha Wilcox was a prominent teacher during the years when the Christian Science organization was at its peak of prosperity. She grew up on a farm in Kansas, under the influence of a religious family life. She studied privately for a Teacher's Certificate and became a teacher in the local schools. Before finding Christian Science, she was an active member of the Methodist Church. It was through a series of events, in which she sought medical aid for her ailing husband, that she was presented in 1902 with a copy of *Science and Health.* As she studied and pondered this book, she was healed of a physical problem of long-standing. While her husband was not interested in Christian Science, she definitely was.

Within the next six years, she had Primary class instruction, became an active member of a branch church in Kansas City, Missouri, and managed to devote much of her time to the healing work, in addition to caring for her family. In 1908 she received a call from The Mother Church in Boston asking her to serve Mrs. Eddy at her home in Chestnut Hill, Massachusetts.

In Mrs. Wilcox's first interview with Mrs. Eddy, it was impressed upon her that everything in one's experience is subjective or mental. Mrs. Wilcox writes of this interview: "[Mrs. Eddy], no doubt, realized that at my stage of growth, I thought of creation — that is, all things — as separated into two groups, one group spiritual and the other group material. But during this lesson I caught my first glimpse of the fact that all right, useful things — which I had been calling 'the unrighteous mammon' — were mental and represented spiritual ideas. She showed me that unless I were faithful and orderly with the objects of sense that made up my present mode of consciousness, there would never be revealed to me the 'true riches,' or the progressively higher revealments of substance and things."

Mrs. Wilcox later wrote: "I well remember when for the first time I understood that everything of which I am conscious is thought, and never external to or separate from what I call my mind, and that which I call my mind is not always seeing things as they actually are."

In 1910, Mrs. Wilcox was recommended by Mrs. Eddy for Normal Class instruction, with Bicknell Young as teacher. This was the beginning of a long and successful career for Mrs. Wilcox as a practitioner and teacher. In 1911, she taught her first class. Until her passing in 1948, she was dedicated to serving the Christian Science movement, and became one of the most respected teachers in the Field. She was the author of many profound papers on Christian Science, mainly papers given each year to her association of students.

Mrs. Wilcox's two years with Mrs. Eddy equipped her to understand so well the subjective nature of all things. She explains how to shift the focal point of thought from the objective world of people, things, happenings, to the subjective world of intuitions, thoughts, ideas. Although she stresses the mental cause of disease and discord, she goes beyond an analysis of the human mind and explains how to relate to God subjectively through prayer; how to develop an understanding of Him that spiritualizes consciousness and heals, how to transcend the false material view of creation and find the spiritual view.

At the time that Mrs. Wilcox wrote these addresses, the Church organization would not permit the publication or circulation of such papers. But Mrs. Wilcox did share them privately with students, and they were handed down over the years to the present time. In giving these papers to her students, it is possible that Mrs. Wilcox hoped they would someday go forth to bless the world, for surely she must have been aware of their timeless message.

For further information regarding Christian Science:
Write: The Bookmark
            Post Office Box 801143
            Santa Clarita, CA 91380
Call: 1-800-220-7767
Visit our website: www. thebookmark.com